Autism, Access and Inclusion
on the Front Line

of related interest

Access and Inclusion for Children with Autistic Spectrum Disorders
'Let Me In'
Matthew Hesmondhalgh and Christine Breakey
Foreword by Richard Exley
ISBN 1 85302 986 6

Asperger Syndrome – What Teachers Need to Know
Matt Winter
Written for Cloud 9 Children's Foundation
ISBN 1 84310 143 2

Specialist Support Approaches to Autism Spectrum Disorder Students in Mainstream Settings
Sally Hewitt
ISBN 1 84310 290 0

Addressing the Challenging Behavior of Children with High-Functioning Autism/Asperger Syndrome in the Classroom
A Guide for Teachers and Parents
Rebecca A. Moyes
ISBN 1 84310 719 8

Freaks, Geeks and Asperger Syndrome
A User Guide to Adolescence
Luke Jackson
Foreword by Tony Attwood
ISBN 1 84310 098 3
Winner of the NASEN & TES Special Educational Needs Children's Book Award 2003

Asperger's Syndrome
A Guide for Parents and Professionals
Second Edition
Tony Attwood
ISBN 1 84310 307 9

Autism, Access and Inclusion on the Front Line

Confessions of an Autism Anorak

Matthew Hesmondhalgh

Foreword by Jacqui Jackson

Jessica Kingsley Publishers
London and Philadelphia

Front cover design by Sinead Fletcher, a pupil in The Resource, and Sallyanne McCann, a member of the staff team.

First published in 2006
by Jessica Kingsley Publishers
116 Pentonville Road
London N1 9JB, UK
and
400 Market Street, Suite 400
Philadelphia, PA 19106, USA

www.jkp.com

Library of Congress Cataloging in Publication Data
Hesmondhalgh, Matthew, 1962-
  Autism, access and inclusion on the front line : confessions of an autism anorak / Matthew Hesmondhalgh ; foreword by Jacqui Jackson.
    p. cm.
  Includes bibliographical references and index.
  ISBN-13: 978-1-84310-393-6 (pbk. : alk. paper)
  ISBN-10: 1-84310-393-1 (pbk. : alk. paper) 1. Autistic youth--Education. 2. Autistic youth--Employment. I. Title.
  LC4717.5.H47 2006
  371.94--dc22

2006005673

British Library Cataloguing in Publication Data
A CIP catalogue record for this book is available from the British Library

ISBN-13: 978 1 84310 393 6
ISBN-10: 1 84310 393 1

Printed and bound in Great Britain by
Athenaeum Press, Gateshead, Tyne and Wear

*For Hamish, and the courage he demonstrates
on a minute-by-minute basis.*

Contents

List of Tables and Figures

Foreword

All I can say is 'Thank God for autism anoraks!' If there were more of them in the world then, as Matthew so bravely states, we would not need to label our children and talk of their 'impairments'. I maintain that communication is a two-way thing, as is social interaction, so surely it is both the misunderstood and the ones misunderstanding that are impaired? My sons may not communicate in quite the same way as many others in the world, they may not interact with others in quite the same way and they are certainly rigid in their thinking, but impaired? In some ways yes but in others I would say they are enhanced. As any mother of seven children, four of whom are on the autistic spectrum, when I think of any of my children I smile to myself instantly and my heart is filled with a warm glow. However, when I think of my boys, the things they have said and done and their own unique way of viewing the world, I can make myself giggle at even my bleakest moments and I am sure all parents of children with an autistic spectrum disorder (ASD) and those working with them can do the same. That is surely something to be treasured.

As a parent of children of all various colours of the autistic spectrum, I may not have worked in a school (and nor would I want to!) but I have certainly spent many frustrating hours speaking to teachers in schools who not only do not 'get it' but do not even want to try. When any of my boys start a new school or a new term I set myself a task: I try to meet as many teachers whom I consider to be 'autism friendly'. Sadly there were too few in the schools that my son Luke attended and so eventually he had to leave school completely and be home educated. I thank God for the autism friendly teachers who helped Luke through the difficult school years and to the members of our complex difficulties team for their support through our tough times, but the stark reality was that between us all we merely managed to keep Luke alive and sane rather than gain him any education or formal qualifications. He is now, at the ripe old age of 17, at college with full-time support from people who listen and care, and is taking 5 GCSEs; something which should have been done at school as he is certainly bright enough. Unfortunately in the schools that he attended, there were not enough, if any, autism anoraks to help him through and the ones that worked for our local education authority were spread too thin to be able to help in a hands-on way.

Luke is now forging his way in the world and learning each day and I am very proud of his ability to negotiate his way through the obstacles of life. However, to read books like this one brings joy to my heart in the knowledge that other children will not have to plough their way through a minefield of bullying and misunderstanding and hit rock bottom before they can even attempt to learn any skills in life or in formal education.

Fortunately for me, things are changing and more and more people like Matthew Hesmondhalgh are surrounding my children and I cannot ever begin to express my gratitude as, I am sure, will be the feelings of the parents of the many young people who have been fortunate to have Matthew and his staff as their teachers and mentors. At present, my son Joe's life and subsequently the life of all of his six siblings and myself, has been turned around by an amazing support worker who, as a parent of a child on the spectrum herself, has decided to use her experience to help children like her son. I wake up each morning feeling as if I have won the lottery as my little boy prepares for school with a smile on his face and looks forward to the day. I hope this book will go some way to educating other teachers and professionals and encouraging parents in the knowledge that autism anoraks are on the increase because without them, life would be inconceivable...

Jacqui Jackson
Author of Multicoloured Mayhem

Introduction

The warmth and encouragement we have received since our first book (Hesmondhalgh and Breakey 2001) has been overwhelming. The fact that people visit our place of work, and come to our conferences from all over the UK is still a cause of much puzzlement for me and the team of staff whom I work alongside. This book may well undo all the goodwill we have appeared to gain over the last four years so I will apologise now to the people with whom I work. Theories and long technical words do not appear in this book. What follows are my opinions and ideas about autism, how far we have come over the past twenty years, and where I think progress has to be made. There are three naked and raw emotions that have prompted this book: joy, anger and fear.

I am unbelievably lucky and privileged. I have driven to work with a smile on my face for the last eleven years. To place 1,200 teenagers in one large building, call it a school, and then expect learning to be the outcome is ambitious to say the least. Secondary schools however good, are places of pure survival for large numbers of our young people today. On top of all the pressures of teenage life today, they are expected to learn, produce their best and behave well. Teachers have my utmost respect. I could not be a 'normal teacher'. The dwindling numbers of people wanting to join the teaching profession does not surprise me. One of the factors, which produces my usual smile, is that in our school there is a resource base full of wonderful people who support and guide twenty-eight pupils with autistic spectrum disorders (ASDs) within this large institution of learning. Make no mistake, I learn more than the children do. They have more to teach than I do. Going to work for me is like going to listen and learn from those great teachers whom you remember from your school days, or those lecturers at college who brought their subject matter to life. The magicians of life and learning. Eleven years ago, faced with the task of establishing a resource base for pupils with ASDs in this busy secondary school, I was not sure whether children on the spectrum would have anything to gain or contribute. The secondary stage of education within mainstream schools is the tough bit. Many of the stories from people with ASDs themselves were ones of battle scars, if not open seeping wounds. Most of the stories in this book are happier than the ones of ten to twenty years ago (and so they should be). Yet nothing we have done in this school is rocket science. To their credit, Sheffield Local Education Authority (LEA) has opened two more resources for pupils with ASDs in mainstream secondary schools. There are plans to open more at both secondary and primary level.

Over the next few years, I fully expect the release of some publications that will claim to be definitive guidebooks in terms of autism. They will most likely be written by very eminent people. I would be most surprised if these experts will have experienced the day-to-day pleasure of working with people on the spectrum for a number of years. The minute non-autistic people step away from practical, regular hands-on work with people who are on the spectrum, they should have less to say. The opposite appears to be true and that seems to be the case in other areas of life, too. Many teachers at our school devoured Mark Haddon's excellent book, *The Curious Incident of the Dog in the Night-time*. It reached the parts other books fail to touch. Many of them recognised the main character in the book and related him to pupils they have taught at school. Books by advocates themselves are invaluable and Luke Jackson stands out as a guiding light in recent years.

Fear and anger are comfortable partners. We have seen great progress in the field of ASDs over the past twenty years. The pockets of excellent work are enough to make a large and colourful patchwork quilt. So many good people, parents, professionals and people with ASDs have given blood, sweat and tears to improve understanding, inclusion and expectations. In the short history of ASDs we are making progress. Diagnosis is improving all the time. Early years education has made great progress. The media has played a role in raising the positive profile of ASDs. However, there is a feeling among a number of people that we have reached something of an impasse. In some ways, the progress made merely serves to highlight how much further we still have to travel.

Where education has progressed, support and understanding from other vital agencies such as Social Services appears to remain in the dark ages. The idea of support in some form being needed from cradle to grave is light years away. This is worrying. People with ASDs are extremely under-represented in the employment market in the UK. In our work with employers, finance has to be sought through charitable means. This is wrong, but highlights some wider issues in society that need to be examined. while this book is being written I will hear about whether or not a National Lottery bid for £100,000 has been successful. This bid has been completed after a day at work. A professional fundraiser and lottery bid 'filler in' will make £150 for checking my bid to see if it is OK. Professional fundraisers and people who specialise at filling in bids for charities are now vital people in our society. That sounds like one of those 'strange but true' facts you get in Christmas crackers. This £100,000 would make our work in supported employment secure for the next three years and enable us to expand and achieve more. On my drive to work, I pass a local cricket pavilion in a wealthy part of Sheffield that has been financed through the National Lottery. I am a big fan of cricket, but I guess you can see why I might be angry about this use of charitable funds. If our bid fails…well, anger and fear working in perfect harmony again. The wonderful people employed by our charity will be out of a job and the support they offer will end. My daughter has one of those postcard slogans on her bedroom wall. 'Wouldn't it be great if all the necessary funding for education and health was provided, and the army had to hold craft fairs to raise money for guns and planes'. Whatever happens with our life line (lottery bid) I promise to let you know at the end of the book.

Parents, professionals and people with ASDs themselves may have changed a small corner of society, but it is a big bad world out there. The people, pressures and ideas which we need to challenge will not change for the better without a struggle. Common sense and reasoned arguments will not be enough. An eminent politician in the UK recently described parents of children with ASDs as the two-fisted street fighters of the disability movement. Strong language but I know what he means. It is time for professionals to stand up and be counted as well. They can no longer smile from their little corners secure in the knowledge that they are doing a good job, or even a great job. It is the wider picture that counts. Investment in education has been good. This covers maybe a quarter of someone's life. We are adults for a lot longer than we are children. It is generally with fear and anger that I view the subsequent three-quarters of life for someone with an ASD.

It is four years since a colleague, Christine Breakey, and I wrote about our little corner of work (Hesmondhalgh and Breakey 2001). Writing parts of this first book was a therapeutic process for me. It was idealistic in places as well as being grounded in good practice. When I talk to fellow 'anoraks' around the country, this idea that we have reached somewhat of an impasse comes through loud and clear. Politicians always point to the pockets of good work, but this might also be a way for them to do little more. They can proudly boast about this bit of work and that project, especially if it happens to be within their constituency. The joined up thinking and 'seamless service' remains elusive and distant. A few still whisper of a postcode lottery.

So what is an 'autism anorak'? For those non-anoraks I will try to explain using simple terminology. Anoraks are often seen at conferences and workshops on autism around the UK. They generally look pale and tired. An anorak will cleverly steer any conversation back to ASDs. Anoraks will attempt to outdo fellow anoraks with practical examples of: good practice, lessons learnt, mistakes made, examples of horrendous mis-management and news of the latest books, research and TV programmes. The autism anorak has an inbuilt respect for fellow practitioners, but a growing mistrust of politicians and academics. Anoraks are either parents, advocates or professionals who work on the front line of public services. As Peeters and Gillberg (1999) point out 'for want of another explanation…one needs to be bitten by the bug of autism. For insiders, this is perfectly clear.' They go on to suggest that 'professionals must choose autism themselves' (p.82). Billions of pounds going into research on autism, while important, will not comfort the anorak who does not know how they will pay for the next ream of paper, or next computer gadget required by a friend on the spectrum whose life will not be worth living unless he has it *now*. Anoraks may disagree about approaches and philosophies but they will listen carefully to each other and usually enjoy each other's company. They may be social outcasts from people in society who do not share or understand their passionate need, in terms of autism, to change things for the better. Autism anoraks usually make friends and opponents in roughly equal quantities.

The autism anoraks know what needs to be done. They know what injustices blight the lives of many people with ASDs. These injustices, and outright discrimination wear down individuals, their parents, and the anoraks. Things have to change if this journey of progress over the last twenty years is to continue. Most people in society (non-anoraks) still do not 'see' people with ASDs and so their learning curve is stuck in the horizontal position. Sadly, anoraks do not get enough opportunities to talk to non-anoraks about ASDs.

Our National Autistic Society (NAS) is held up to be a mammoth organisation of the great and the good. I cannot imagine where we might be today if it were not for the brilliance of a few people within the NAS, especially parents. But a National Society that represents all? Not sure about that one. Certainly a very wealthy charity with some expensive schools to run. For those areas of the UK it cannot adequately cover, the private sector is more than happy to compete for funds from LEAs and Social Services. Still, it was great news when a huge private telecommunications company pledged to raise £6 million for our National Society over a three-year period. Sadly, our work does not fall under the auspices of the NAS. It is not difficult to guess what effect that has had on our little applications for funding to charities and trust funds. These were not bids for vast sums of money. One such application was for £5000, for example. Hence the National Lottery bid. Let us hope that the National Lottery people understand that not everyone with ASDs will benefit from this huge injection of money into an already wealthy organisation.

'Hold on!' I hear you cry, this is only the introduction and the author is already a marked man having added considerably to his list of critics/opponents. Let me return to language that will not make the publisher's legal department quiver with fear and trepidation.

This book will examine our current thinking and experiences in education, employment and supported living. It is based on what Americans call action research (i.e. 'doing' and learning rather than thinking about it). Mistakes continue to be made on a daily basis and there is a deep beauty in the inevitable nature of this (if you look hard enough, and after a few drinks). However, this book will aim to do more. Autism has to be placed within the wider framework and context of what is actually happening in our schools, places of employment and society as a whole. The team of people I work alongside continually tell visitors to our school that this is not rocket science. Many of the ideas and suggestions put forward in this book are remarkably simple. Staff are trying to support others in understanding the fundamental challenges associated with autism. As Patricia Howlin says (1997) 'the focus is not on "cures" or "miracles" but on the improvement in the quality of life for all concerned' (p.7).

It may upset and anger some parents, people with ASDs and professionals. This is not my aim, although I do feel it is time to 'shake things up a bit'. After an enjoyable but tiring day at work, a couple of hours trying to raise finance for our employment projects, and perhaps another fund-raising activity to plan, it is easy to be cynical. I recently met three dedicated Autism Support Workers who have to attempt to raise awareness and work with pupils on the spectrum in nurseries, primary and secondary schools in the county of Norfolk. This is a huge area to cover without the aid of a small aeroplane. I was in awe of their commitment, energy and determination to change things for the better. However, they were also tired. Anoraks are allowed to be a little cynical sometimes, but they tend to be overwhelmingly positive people who occasionally get tired and depressed about the lack of good provision. There are not enough people on the front line doing the nitty gritty day-to-day things that do make a difference. There are too many injustices on the front line to be simply brushed aside as isolated examples. There is too much waste in the system to allow things to carry on as they are. The West

Indian culture has a saying: 'there is no justice in the world, just us'. It is time for anoraks to stand up one more time and be counted. There are people, issues and ideas to confront, and we are only strong enough for the next part of the journey if we stand together.

When my professional life as an autism anorak is over, I will have nothing more to say on the subject (that is a promise). I shall cycle, read, spend time with my family and discuss other subject matter. Until that day, it is time to give the ball another kick. I apologise in advance to those who may read this and take offence. I usually prefer to be like Marlon Brando in *The Godfather* and keep my friends close but my enemies closer still. But, these are tough times on the front line. The anoraks may need some help.

CHAPTER 1

Are We Nearly There Yet?

Andrew and Shaun were the first two pupils with a recognised ASD who stepped into King Ecgbert secondary school to receive our magical support and guidance. There was nothing vaguely magical or mysterious about the emotions we all felt at this time. These emotions ranged from fear to shock and back again, on a minute-by-minute basis. As all three of us walked down the bustling main corridor at school and realised that the most important skills were those possessed by good rugby players, the uppermost thought in my mind was to remain in our purpose-built resource base (the only problem being, it was not built yet). Andrew and Shaun were going to be severely damaged both physically and mentally, of that I was in no doubt.

Quick. Who was the most picked on kid in your year at secondary or high school? Right, exactly, you can recall that name, first and last. You can picture them. You might remember watching 'an incident' or them walking home alone. Whatever you remember, that name stays with you. Is it worse today than when you were at school? That is too important a debate for so early in this book. The parents of Shaun and Andrew had put tremendous faith in me. For 'faith in', read 'pressure on'. There was no way that either of them could become that 're-membered name'. There were hearts and minds to be won and eleven years later, this process still goes on. The difference today is that for a twenty-place resource, the eleven staff support twenty-eight pupils. It is a human process not bound by theories, class, or rigid principles. We could not demand good inclusive attitudes from the mainstream peers of Shaun and Andrew. Most of them were frightened little Year 7 (Y7) children themselves. All their energies were being invested in looking after number one. They had to see and learn that being 'different' is more than just all right. Being different should have its own exam course the same as Dance, English and Performing Arts. Difference should be the cause of celebration and delight. The fact that we have not reached such a simplistic obvious truth is not the fault of education or teachers.

Openness with these young impressionable minds was one of the ways to make progress. In fact it is the only way. When you want someone to understand more about something, you have to explain the little bit that you know. You have to share some knowledge. You have to be prepared to answer some questions, usually difficult ones. This involves an element of risk. Our education system has not yet prevented children from being generally inquisitive. But the key is, you have to admit when you have not got 'the answer'. Questions without answers are uncomfortable in secondary education. At the same time as this, you have to (trendy, theoretical word coming up – you have been warned) *empower* people to join you in the search for the range of possible answers. You demand that people join you on this journey of exploration, but make it appear like an invitation to a lifelong party they cannot afford to miss. We had pupils and teachers to invite. Most were reluctant and inactive participants in the early years. They had no idea that 'the answers' lay dormant in each of them.

During a parents' evening, another of our pupils praised the skills of his History teacher and told him it was not his fault that he had to teach the most boring subject in the curriculum. This is the kind of party where you have to be prepared to play a lot of 'truth or dare' type games. All good honest fun, but a little scary at the same time. Having walked ten miles in the school's gruelling sponsored annual slog, one pupil leaned on my shoulder and gasped, 'Mr Matthew I love you'. I had not got a good trusting relationship with this girl and so was taken aback with the simple beauty of the comment. The basking in my moment of glory was cut short. She went on to elaborate that this new found love was in no way sexual in nature, it was just that she was glad I was there to (quite literally) lean on. The only appropriate response was a period of silent reflective meditation. This is the kind of party where there is no quizmaster, nobody in charge of food and drinks, and nobody to say when it is time to get your coat and leave.

Andrew and Shaun and their peers had a great five years at secondary school. Socially, they grew with their peers. Shaun in particular did not want to miss out on anything. He threw himself into History, Maths and Science with the same infectious enthusiasm as lunchtime choir practice and Christmas concerts. Andrew began to see that he did have skills that would be appreciated and that his great knowledge of *Star Wars* or *The Simpsons* gave him a lot to take to 'the party'. There were bits they did not like, but that is true for everyone. Hands up those of you who enjoyed all subjects in school?

Recently, I did a talk in Harrogate about our work. A delegate asked some really insightful (for insightful, read tough) questions around counselling her son about his autism. My answers were burbled and inadequate. When she approached me afterwards I got the apologies in quickly. She quickly brushed my words aside. She told me that she had left the teaching profession a little disillusioned and had spent time at home with her family. On the strength of reading our first book, she had returned to the profession and had gone for a job to set up a resource base in a secondary school where she lived, for pupils with ASDs. Eleven years ago, we were all petrified because the party was small and the music quiet. The OFSTED inspector in our first year was brave enough to concede that he had no idea where we would be in four years' time at the next inspection. The frightening thing was, as I sat in the corner with my paper plate of nibbles and cup of fizzy wine, neither did I.

One of the things that appeared to worry the powers that be was that Shaun and Andrew, and pupils in their wake, would bring down the academic results of the school. All pupils in The Resource at King Ecgbert School have a Statement of Special Educational Needs. In most accepted terms, this means that their autism is severe. (The words 'mild' and 'autism' must never appear in the same sentence.) I had not considered the work and commitment needed to be successful at GCSEs. For me this success might be what others consider lower grades in these national exams. That would be all right, because it would represent the best possible efforts of an individual pupil. Over the years, pupils with ASDs at the school have had some lovely successes at GCSE level. About 30 per cent of the pupils gain three or more GCSEs at C grade or above. About 60 per cent gain one C grade. This appeared to worry a school where in a bad year, the success rate for pupils who gain five or more grades at GCSE of C or above stands at about 55 per cent.

Legally, schools have to include all pupils in their exam statistics. Statisticians are usually people I do not like to invite to a party. However, when statisticians began to talk about 'value added' stuff, they suddenly became the life and soul of the party. Staff in The Resource were dealing with the two curricula someone with an ASD needs, the academic one and the social one. Over a five-year period the value added bit would be a reflection of how good the school is, but also a measure of success of 'our approaches'. This idea was even better in some respects because the testing at the start of secondary school life was hard and the pupils were only just settling in. Our pupils should score badly because of the new experience of a 'blind test', exam conditions, fear of making mistakes and just the injustice of being tested for no apparent reason or reward. Sadly, this is not always the case, and some pupils on the spectrum score well on the non-verbal reasoning tests. This should not surprise us.

The problem is that as human beings, we know it is unfair to put some 11-year-old pupils through the potentially damaging experience of formal testing so early in their schooling. Value judgements have to be made and therefore, mistakes are made. Shaun and Andrew sat the tests (then called NFER tests) and did very badly. It took Andrew a long time to recover from the shock of silent exam conditions, and me a long time to overcome the feelings of guilt. Pupils do not even get to know how well they have done. I felt like a party pooper who has to get his coat and leave early. Today, these tests have developed into sophisticated booklets that examine verbal and non-verbal skills and logical thought processes. They are now called CAT tests and take approximately three hours (over a two-day period). From these tests, the school predicts what each pupil can expect to get five years later in their GCSE exams. Brilliant. We try to get all our pupils to take these tests, but for a small number, it would be cruel and pointless.

Table 1.1 looks at these figures for the last four years. It is not included to make our work and our pupils 'look good'. It is included to show that academic success should be considered a given when appropriate support is available for pupils with ASDs. The results of the fifteen pupils in the table are a reflection of their hard work and determination, good teaching and skilled support. They still need to be better.

Three of the pupils in the table are now in the school's sixth form doing A levels or their equivalent. These three lads are the first to stay on with us. Two of the three pupils in the sixth form have exams com-

Table 1.1 NFER scores, predicted and actual grades at GCSEs for the years 2001–2004

Pupil	Average NFER scores at Y7	5 A–C grade	Overall grades *expected*	*Actual* GCSE grades 5 years later
1	118	Yes	B	4 Bs, 3 Cs and 1 D grade
2	93	No	E	1 B and 7 C grades
3	73	No	X (no grade)	1 C, 2 Ds, 3 Es and 1 F grade
4	81	No	F	3 F grades
5	92.5	No	E	1 B and 6 C grades
6	74	No	X	1 C, 1 D, 3 Es and 2 F grades
7	69.5	No	X	1 D, 1 E and 4 F grades
8	82.5	No	F	1 C, 2 Ds and 4 E grades
9	78.5	No	G	2 Es, 5 Fs and 1 G grade
10	69	No	X	2 G grades
11	95.5	No	D	1 C and 6 D grades
12	71.5	No	X	2 Ds, 2 Es and 1 F grade
13	73	No	X	1 D, 1 E, 2 Fs and 1 G grade
14	85.5	No	F	3 Cs, 2 Ds and 4 E grades
15	108.5	Yes	C	1 B, 6 Cs and 1 D grade

ing up so I went to see the exams officer to discuss arrangements with him. He had forgotten about pupils with ASDs doing A level exams and was very apologetic. He is a good person and had no need to apologise. The same man is the first person to celebrate exam success at GCSEs when the results come out in August. I like to be at school on that day to watch the looks of delight and pride. It is good when parents turn up to support their sons and daughters as well. I do have to work hard at giving nothing away because I am privileged enough to learn the results from our exams officer the day before they are officially released to the pupils.

There are no hard and fast rules in terms of subjects which suit and subjects which should be avoided. We have small successes in Modern Foreign Languages, Technologies such as Textiles, Food and Resistant Materials, History and at PE GCSE. English grades in language and literature are a little lower than other subjects but in the four years represented by the table, only one of those pupils has failed to deliver a C grade in either of these two tough subjects. Shaun got his C grade in English Literature and devoured the book *Of Mice And Men* by John Steinbeck. In doing so he taught staff yet again, that anything is possible and expectations need to be high, even verging on the ridiculous.

Where there is advice on teaching, it is better given by those teachers who found it easy to include pupils with ASDs into their classrooms and subject areas. Tom is a brilliant History teacher in a very strong department at King Egbert School. He has seen The Resource grow from nothing and has worked with many colleagues from the team. He taught Shaun and Andrew for two years. Shaun went on to do GCSE and achieved a remarkable D grade. Recently we have been delighted to include Tom in some training sessions for staff at the school, and for delegates who attended one of our conferences. I just sit back in his lessons and watch all children learn to love History. The following words and advice are his:

> I often like to use acrostics in my teaching of History, especially for lower school pupils. It aids recall and is a good practical and fun way for children to learn. Using the word 'resource' I have devised an acrostic to show what factors and techniques are

important to me in teaching history to mainstream pupils and those on the autistic spectrum. Mike Collins who is an education advisor to the NAS believes that good teaching practice for children with autism is good practice for other children too.

- Range of techniques to present work
- Enjoyment
- Showing an interest in pupils in other situations
- Orderly working environment
- Understanding of the pupils
- Rigorous – but also realistic – targets
- Clear, concise instructions
- Examples of good, challenging practice

In my opinion, it is important to use a range of techniques for the presentation of work. Pupils must be taught and encouraged to take pride in all work they attempt. There should be a variety of techniques to suit each pupil. These could include: bullet point summaries, evidence jigsaws (e.g. pieces that fit together to help us find out about the Romans), gap filling/sentence completion, audiotape presentations (e.g. radio report of the execution of Charles I), postcards, spider diagrams and speech bubbles.

My tutor at university gave a good illustration to remind student teachers that learning should be enjoyable:

> There is a large, beautiful and majestic fish in a glass tank. The tank is separated in the middle by a glass panel, which prevents the fish getting into the part of its tank that contains its favourite food supply – a particular kind of smaller fish. The fish can see its prey but keeps swimming into the glass partition. This continues for days until the fish is exhausted, confused and demoralised. The glass panel is lifted from the tank and the fish can now get to its small prey. However, it leaves them alone. It has been conditioned to miss out. The fish remains forlorn in his original half of the tank and does not venture near the smaller fish.

I determined very early in my training that I had to make it a priority to ensure that my pupils did not miss out.

History can be fun, especially the horrible, funny and 'stranger than fiction' bits. Pupils in Year 7 love the fact that ladies dipped their handkerchiefs in the blood of Charles I after his execution, or that blackbird was a favourite Roman delicacy.

I often visit The Resource base in school to see staff and pupils. As Head of Lower School it is part of my role to show an interest in pupils in a variety of settings such as sports day, school drama productions and social events.

My classroom is an orderly working environment. There are simple ground rules for everyone. Learning does not happen efficiently if the classroom is a noisy and chaotic environment. Sometimes, with a particular project or piece of work, it can be beneficial for pupils with an ASD to work in their base. This occurs during times of research or model making for example. I have to attempt to understand the needs of thirty pupils in a class, their strengths and weaknesses and what is their absolute best. For pupils with an ASD, my dialogue with staff from The Resource is vital in this process. I get a written outline of additional needs with useful information on it, but the suggestions and guidance from staff skilled in this area of work makes my life much easier. The aim is to be able to set rigorous but realistic targets for each pupil so that they are stretched and challenged within their own range of strengths and weaknesses.

My verbal teaching must be backed up by a written summary whenever possible. Written directions whether on a paper handout or whiteboard, should be neat and attractive with an appropriate reading content. In Upper School, our department uses two textbooks at GCSE, a slightly easier one in terms of reading content, and another book with a higher reading content. Homework must be written in planners to maintain a line of communication with parents and support staff who may not have been in the lesson. There is little point in giving out homework right at the end of a lesson and expecting good quality work to come back from pupils.

Classrooms need to have good examples of work on walls and models on display. It is important to celebrate success and to maintain a thread of surprise, challenge and wonder throughout the school year. In Y7 our pupils do an open project on Roman life. Some pupils make Roman food like custards and rich cakes. These provide a happy and entertaining tasting lesson for pupils and staff alike.

Having a staff who are skilled and experienced in the field of autism has made my introduction to this complex disability relatively easy. The training offered has been good and it is a genuine two-way relationship with staff and pupils from The Resource. I asked staff from The Resource to outline how my teaching methods helped pupils with an ASD to learn. Some of their direct quotes can be found in Figure 1.1.

Tom Smiles, History teacher at King Ecgbert School

I have been supporting in Tom's History lessons for the last eleven years and I still learn something new each time a topic is taught. The new whiteboard technology will always be utilised well by teachers such as Tom, although his blackboard displays were works of art in themselves. However, none of what Tom has written about is revolutionary stuff in terms of teaching, education and autism. Staff supporting pupils with ASDs are lucky at King Ecgbert School to find this standard of teaching and classroom management on a regular basis. It is not difficult to imagine lessons of the opposite kind to those based on the advice and guidance from Tom. Again, this is relatively simple advice based largely on common sense and hard work.

I have met Andrew several times in recent months. When Andrew was at school, the best part of his week was the morning he spent on work placement at Sainsbury's supermarket. while at college, Andrew started getting paid for working at Sainsbury's. With support from a member of staff funded through our charity (King Ecgbert Resource, registered number 1068541), he took an exam in food safety and hygiene so that he could progress to serving on the bakery counter. He passed a Level 1 and a Level 2 GNVQ (General National Vocational Qualification) in Retail work (the equivalent of

Figure 1.1 Autism in the History classroom

GCSEs at C grade or above). Andrew now works for roughly twenty hours a week at Sainsbury's.

On a social evening just before Christmas, organised for the young adults we know, Andrew was telling me about all the overtime he was being asked to do during the busy festive period. Andrew would not have entertained the very idea of overtime a few years ago, but now he thought that the extra money could come in useful. He chatted to his friends, some of whom he had not seen for a year. Andrew and his friends played pool together. These evenings are great fun for all involved and it is a great shame that we cannot organise them on a more regular basis. There are only twenty-four hours in a day and I am always grateful to staff who regularly attend such evenings. How many other front line service providers can say that they see the results of all their hard work over the years? It does not make any sense to me that our expertise and dedication should end just because someone is aged sixteen or eighteen. It is equally nonsensical that other service providers (if they exist) then begin to support a young adult and possibly run the risk of making the same mistakes over again. Too many different agencies are currently involved in the life of someone with an ASD and the 'overview' and the person themselves, are in danger of being lost in the processes. I love to spend time with Andrew (now in his twenties) because I go back to school the next day with renewed determination and energy. I am re-assured that our bungling and often naive attempts to provide what Andrew needed have helped to produce a calm, hard-working, fun-loving and sociable young man who is taking his rightful place in society.

I recently found myself at Meadowhall, which is a huge out-of-town shopping/entertainment centre. I know my way round the place a little better now because our charity has had an Employment Support Manager based at the centre since 2003. However, it still remains one of my least favourite places. On this day I was being dragged around by one of my daughters when I saw Andrew queuing at a fast food outlet. It was lunchtime and the queue was long and not particularly orderly. Some customers knew what they wanted and others were milling around trying to view the overhead illuminated menus such places have. There was a lot of noise and several bored and disruptive young children and teenagers. Andrew got into a suitable position to view the menu by asking people if they were in the queue or not. He waited patiently and was very polite with other customers. The whole 'social scene' was one of general disorder, but Andrew took his time and assessed each situation on its merits and as he saw it. Nobody looked at Andrew in a disgruntled or overly tolerant way. He was just another person trying to get through this challenging lunchtime situation. I was so proud of him.

But, are we nearly there yet? Our Y11 pupils (aged 15 to 16 years old) are beginning the vital process of examining their options for post-16 education. We have forged good links with Sheffield College over the last few years. The management and lecturers at this college have gone from having little knowledge or expertise in the field of autism to developing a growing service in terms of support and guidance for students with ASDs. One of our Y11 pupils would like to follow a course in performing arts at post-16. Sheffield College did not have a suitable course for him so we have made contact with another post-16 provider in Sheffield. This relatively new college has a brilliant course in performing arts that would undoubtedly suit this particular young man. He has been involved in five or six school drama productions and has attended many rehearsals, some of which were during his valuable weekend time. His application form, personal statement and reference from school are very good. A phone call to this college to arrange a visit time and discuss this young man put the whole move into doubt. The college were pleased that he was going to apply but dubious about how much expertise or support they could offer. A comment from the manager of learning support at the college was that they have never had a student on the autistic spectrum before. That is just one indication of how far we have come. First, I do not believe that claim, second, what quality of support have students with ASDs been receiving at this college before and finally, what kind of a statement is that to make from a senior manager anyway? I am not sure how someone can become a manager of learning support and not know a single thing about autism. Reporting this back to the young man's father was not an easy thing to do.

I am confident that every anorak and every person with an ASD and their family members can cite several examples like this one. These examples still anger me. More importantly, I am going to be reluctant to recommend this college to a young man whom we have seen grow and flourish over the past five years at school. However, if this young man still chooses to attend this college we will endeavour to work with the staff there so that they can develop their knowledge and expertise about autism in general, and this young man in particular. More time, energy and resources to ensure that one young man can continue with good quality access and inclusion within an institution of learning that needs to wake up and smell the coffee. I am sure that this post-16 provider is the rule rather than an exception. Even the good providers are sometimes powerless to get things right.

Dominic left King Ecgberts with a bagful of C grades and one B grade at GCSE. The support needed to achieve at this level from both school and parents was quite high. Dominic was very attached to staff in The Resource and to ease his transition to college it was decided that in terms of academic content, he would do an easy course (NVQ in Office and Administration Skills Level 1). Dominic continued to flourish and often returned to The Resource to tell staff about his progress. At the end of this first year at college, Dominic decided that he wanted a more work-based experience. He was accepted on a Modern Apprenticeship in IT at the same college. This would provide work, money and further qualifications. Dominic duly attended the enrolment day at the start of term along with twenty of his peers who had also been accepted on the Modern Apprenticeship. They were all told that the businesses involved who had promised support and work placements had pulled out over the summer months and that the course would not be running. Dominic is still waiting for an apology. The effects on Dominic are not hard to imagine. His mother contacted The Resource and we were able to get Dominic into the Sixth Form at school to do a Vocational Certificate in Education, which is equivalent to two AS Levels. He has worked hard since then and should pass this course. Ten months later, such is Dominic's anger and bitterness, that he insisted I 'name and shame' this particular college. Not possible. Sorry Dominic.

The fact that our work at school can be undone quickly should surprise no one. The fact that it does happen undermines all the work, time and investment that is occurring in our schools. Pressure to ensure that this does not happen needs to come from people with far more influence than me. The Resource was inspected by Sheffield LEA in July 2003 and by the Office for Standards in Education (OFSTED) in March 2004. (How unlucky was that?) Below, are some of the comments from these inspectors. They are included because people such as these inspectors need to be more involved in ensuring that investment in our education system does not go to waste in later life. We will not be able to ensure that services are in place from cradle to grave until such people play more of a dual role of inspectors and advocates for change. They know what is good and what needs to improve based on their breadth of experience. We know what we do is all right. We know that what comes after education for someone with an ASD is far from all right. This is just one example of the kind of people that anoraks need, to help change things for the better.

What OFSTED said about The Resource, March 2004

- 'Pupils with Autistic Spectrum Disorders benefit strongly from the school's provision and achieve well.'

- 'Pupils with ASDs are withdrawn for lessons directly aimed at their main barrier to learning; their difficulties in relating to other people, and their personal and social skills. Staff have very good knowledge of how to approach this aspect of their learning and they build good and positive relationships that boost pupils' learning tremendously.'

- 'They receive very good explanations or extra work so that their understanding becomes embedded.'

- 'Pupils benefit greatly from extended placements as part of their curriculum, where they have great interest, are learning well, and may develop the opportunity into future paid employment.'

- 'Staff may be in daily contact with parents, perhaps through email between pupils' homes to teachers' homes, or using Dictaphones as a daily diary.'

- 'For autistic pupils the planning is more outward-looking.'

- 'In a Textiles lesson pupils from The Resource were well integrated and achieving highly because of their own high level of motivation and the support of staff.'

What LEA Inspectors said about The Resource, July 2003

- 'The Integrated Resource operates as a separate department within school. This is a key factor in ensuring resources are used to maximum effect. The relationship is symbiotic, with a sharing of benefits and experience.'

- 'The curriculum provided is well adapted to the needs of the pupils and their issues are managed sensitively and intelligently.'

- 'The provision places great emphasis on equality, independence and employment.'

- 'The Head of The Resource is justifiably allowed considerable discretion in its management and development. The Head Teacher has correctly identified the best way to get the best out of his manager.'

- 'Support staff demonstrate a very high level of expertise.'

Staff in the team get a real boost from reports such as these. There is not enough praise and encouragement for people working in front line services from their managers. Yet these front line workers are exactly the people who need to be inspired enough to apply their thinking, planning and practice to change things for the better. I have worked in some special schools where the overwhelming majority of staff do just the acceptable amount of work. Little extra is done because this added value would not have been recognised by senior managers. The chasm between senior managers and their staff who do the 'hands-on' work can be great, including one head teacher who often kept his office door locked if too many children were interrupting his day. This came largely through fear of the children. What a message to give to his staff. It is up to managers to create an atmosphere and ethos where staff feel that anything is possible. I have been lucky enough to work for some great head teachers who gave room for creative thinking and were there to praise, advise or commiserate when needed. However, it is difficult to be creative in today's education system and it appears to be a challenge to actually find good teachers in some subjects. One thing that annoys me is to see older teachers who have officially retired (and perhaps taken an enhanced pension) coming back into schools to offer cover for absent staff. However, if the profession does not attract enough young graduates, then the problems are self-evident.

In terms of autism, teachers have it easy. Financially, they are adequately rewarded. The genuine backbone of services to people with ASDs are the support workers in schools, colleges, Social Services and the voluntary sector. These people, many of whom are anoraks, take home a ridiculously low level of financial reward. Many good support workers have more common sense, dedication, energy and desire to change things for the better than their relatively well-paid teaching colleagues. The salaries for support workers in The Resource currently range from £11,000 pa to £16,500. As a teacher working alongside this body of professional people, I am ashamed and angered by their level of pay. Several of our team of support workers are mothers of young children. Our LEA has just reminded all staff in schools that days taken off work to look after ill dependants must be done so as unpaid leave. What an insult to an already undervalued profession. A more cohesive and organised body of people could bring the vast majority of services to people with ASDs to a standstill if they withdrew their labour. In the meantime, more services must look to improve the working conditions and salaries of support workers. Our charity currently pays a small additional salary to two support workers within the team. This makes me feel less guilty for asking them to take on extra responsibilities such as organising conferences and visitor days. All support workers in The Resource and their colleagues in special schools deserve a higher level of salary.

Anoraks in this field do run a huge risk of becoming seen in a certain way by some people, especially parents. On more than one occasion I have been greeted at a conference as being some kind of hero or saint. Nothing could be further from the truth (ask my wife). But, some people persist in this myth-making, whereby just because you work with a 'disadvantaged' group in society, then it follows that you must also be patient, caring and dedicated. This must follow because there are so many sacrifices involved in being an anorak on the front line. It is not me who wants to make these sacrifices, it is a system that creates 'disadvantaged' groups of people across the board that ensures anoraks like me continue to do more than perhaps we should.

I have had the great misfortune to travel through the centre of London during rush hour on a couple of recent occasions. People were crammed into dirty, noisy trains and forced to invade each other's personal space. Some of them probably boarded the same train five times a week going to the city centre, and then five times home again at the end of their working day. No disrespect to them but some people on these trains looked more tired and more 'grey' than I did. These kinds of people make sacrifices everyday, stifling their own needs, wants and dreams in order to provide for those they love. How much choice some of them had in this process I am not sure about. I chose to do something more exciting, something I love to do. For that, some people think I am 'a good guy'. But, here's the rub. People who work with the disadvantaged, the victimised and the disabled are usually more selfish than anyone. We are not willing to sacrifice our needs. Working at a job that provides for our families is not quite enough. We need personal satisfaction. Some of the people in suits I witnessed on those rush hour trains must hate what they do, but they do it anyway. They do it to provide a better life for themselves and their loved ones. So, who can say which of us is to be admired? This anorak has taken months to write this book: hundreds of hours away from his family.

One thing that helps us better to assess where we are today in terms of ASDs is the great emphasis on facts and figures. I really have changed my opinion of the people who work these things out. Knapp and Jarbrink 2001 estimated that that the average lifetime costs, from cradle to grave, for someone with an ASD (and associated learning difficulty) is almost three million pounds. For someone with high functioning autism, the cost was estimated at £784,785. I am not good with large numbers but that does sound like a lot of money to me. However, I am not sure where all this money is going, or if it is being invested wisely. With that amount of money, I would have thought that a range of quality, seamless support services from infancy to old age should not be out of the question for every person with an ASD. The fact that this scenario does not exist for the majority of people with an ASD suggests we have many miles yet to travel. I continue to be confused as to why this is the case. Some of these long-term costs of autism could easily be reduced by investment in support services. This investment must be aimed at enhancing the outcomes for social inclusion and independent living. As Patricia Howlin says (1997), 'a focus on the prevention of problems will undoubtedly be more productive than the fruitless search for cures' (p.269). As a non-economist, I can imagine that the number of parents or carers who may want to go back to work, or at least work longer hours, must be quite high. If I was a betting man, I would say that the reduction in any benefits claimed would not be the major barrier in achieving this. People are basically good. However, parents cannot work if there are inadequate care facilities available.

Logical, rational and patient arguments are not going to achieve a great deal anymore. While Social Services across the country dither and choke on the term 'investment in services', the private sector rubs its hands in glee. Maybe I am wrong. Maybe three million is not a lot to pay.

CHAPTER 2

The Triad of Blah, Blah, Blah

We held a conference last year and I had to talk for an hour to 150 people who wanted to know more about our work and our way of thinking. For me, this is never something that gets any easier. Talking to people about something in which you have invested time, effort and tears is always a challenge. It is also a quick cure for constipation. My wonderful colleagues were present and willing me on. My wife and daughter were there as well, hearing me speak in public for the first time. No pressure then. Behind me, on the stage, were large black and white photographs of all the pupils. Some ex-pupils who are now in paid employment, were in the audience. When Hans Asperger wrote that we have a duty to speak out for these people with the whole force of our personalities, I took it literally. I also know how lucky and privileged I am. My granddad told me there are two types of people in the world, those who want to be a somebody, and those who want to do something. The chance to do something landed in my lap. I was in the right place at the right time. With the benefit of hindsight, I have enjoyed every mistake. The people with whom I have worked, those with ASDs and those without, have generally been brilliant. The pupils continue to inspire me onto the next struggle. They give me the voice with which to speak out.

I do not recognise any of my friends in relation to the triad of impairments. My criticisms of the triad are not aimed at the pioneers who thought of it and used it as an aid to help improve the understanding of others. My criticisms are merely at the length of time it has existed. How many other disabilities do we begin by talking about what a group of people might find more challenging? Every one of my friends has strengths and abilities I can list. Some of the strengths of some of my friends make me envious. Each of them has something to teach me, usually when I am least expecting it. Yet, I still go to conferences and workshops where the triad is held up at the start as 'The Model'. It would be confined to the past if only we could come up with something better. Luke Jackson, who describes himself beautifully as having a 'grasshopper mind', draws the analogy between the triad (plus repetitive behaviours, obsessions and sensory problems) and a graphic equaliser. The idea is that all people on the autistic spectrum have different levels for each of the challenging areas. This is certainly an improvement in explaining the idea of a spectrum. But, it still misses the point. There is no model to fit human beings, on the spectrum or not on it. Having said that, I have spent minutes (literally) developing my own model, which you can see on the next page. This is my Tridecagon of Impairments. For those of you who are non-mathematicians, a Tridecagon is a thirteen-sided shape. Mine has emerged into the loose shape of a bird and the adding of an eye could be crucial. I now intend to travel the country to talk about this simple model and attempt to apply it to all the other 1 in every 166 people who are a bit like me. Books, lecture tours and a website will follow. I shall make my fortune and retire to a small uninhabited island off the coast of Norway.

The Triad of Blah, Blah, Blah is a dismissive term I know. It is not mine, but a wonderful young man called DJ who went through some tough times learning about and accepting his autism when he was fourteen. Now in his third year at college doing advanced level IT, DJ is a brilliant role model for some of our young pupils at school. He has learned about, objected to and now accepted his autism through taking a journey of self-discovery. His autism is part of his wonderful self, and he values those people who can accept him for who he is, and ignores the rest.

Someone at a conference (probably an anorak) reminded me that we have 'the iceberg model'. You know the science – icebergs being nine-tenths hidden below the waterline with only one-tenth

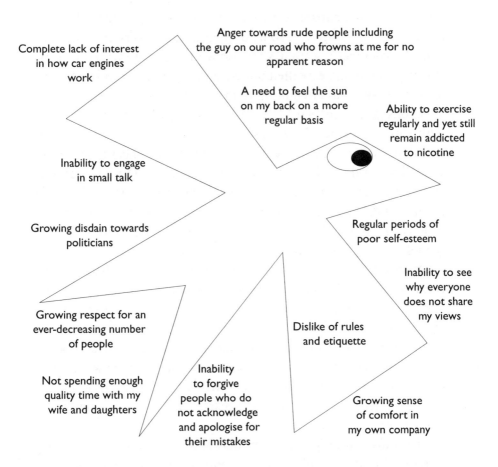

Figure 2.1 A tridecagon of impairments

showing. I fail to understand this model on two counts. First, I do not work in an environment where autism is hidden away. Staff spend a lot of time talking to pupils within The Resource about their autism. Strengths are focused on, along with areas that could be developed. These are my friends, but I have to tell you that the majority of them do not hide their autism away. They are also going through the adolescent bit and along with some of their teenage peers, they are very much 'in your face'. Second, staff also work very hard with the mainstream pupils to increase their understanding of this complex disability. Last week I was attempting to explain to a group of twenty-five Y7 pupils (aged between 11 and 12 years old) why a particular pupil with autism puts her fingers in her ears at certain times and places within the school day. You will not be surprised to hear that they all wanted to learn and increase their understanding. The question was an honest one and I hope my answer was in the same style. Most pupils appeared to empathise and sympathise with the course of action this pupil took, and a good discussion followed about how the school could improve 'difficult times' for all children.

It should be time to question models and inflexible theories concerning ASDs and get down to the complex issues of learning from, and supporting individuals of whom society has not yet seen the best by a long way. I would like to think we have been doing this for the past eleven years first in an environment that is tough – a secondary school, and second during what can be a challenging period of time for anyone – the teenage bit. I recently heard a friend describe his daughter's teenage bit as 'the dark years'. No explanation necessary, at least not to parents of teenagers.

To throw away inflexible models and theories remains a scary thing to do in any walk of life. It can take away certainty and tick charts. The pupils with ASDs at school have an Annual Review of their Statement of Special Educational Needs. Each review requires a fifteen-page document to be completed for the LEA. In one section, targets have to be set for the coming year (and a simple yes/no box has to be ticked for the previous year's targets). Meetings with parents follow and these discussions about progress are always useful. The document then gets sent to the LEA and someone is paid to look at it. I then get a computer generated letter thanking me (or my colleague) for ticking the right boxes. Half of these letters come to me with a common string of complaints. The targets set are not specific enough, not able to be assessed appropriately or not recordable enough.

Many of the targets we set for pupils are general ones for example, 'Fred will settle into a new year at school'. Good target and quite specific. I have not invented a method of recording how staff will teach Fred to do this, nor do we set measurable criteria so that his 'settling in' can be monitored and recorded. I guess we could do this administrative task, but then we would be spending less time supporting Fred to settle in to his new year at school. How do staff know when Fred has achieved this target? They just do. And so does Fred. I am privileged to work alongside a first rate team of staff. If I gave them a list of criteria to teach and then tick off when Fred had reached a given success rate, they would leave. They work in The Resource because of the thrill of pushing the boundaries back, not to create new ones.

Some of our target setting is not for the pupil but rather for us neurotypicals. For example, 'we will attempt to arrange a work experience placement in a tattoo parlour'. If that is what a pupil would like to do for work experience, we have a duty to at least look into the possibility. Our old dilapidated school, based on two sites (with a road in between) was due to be knocked down and replaced by a brand new building (all on one site) by Easter. All of our pupils had an aim for that Spring and Summer term of, 'to cope with the changes involved in settling into a new building'. This is a crucial aim and a very real one. The letters that come from the LEA are always filed away somewhere really safe. One of the nicest things our LEA has done for us over the past four years since our first book was published is just to leave staff alone so that we can get on with the job. We should have a twenty-place resource in the school. Staff and the management of the school have continually agreed to go 'over numbers'. We currently support twenty-eight pupils. I struggle to turn children away, but I have to consider my stress levels, and those of my colleagues. We try supporting our LEA whenever they want us to take extra pupils, and if they then leave us alone, I consider that a fair trade.

There was no model to help staff prepare pupils for our move into the new building, and what was right for one pupil was not appropriate for the next. This means mistakes were made and learnt from. What we had was a group of staff who were knowledgeable and experienced with the pupils they supported. Staff knew it would be a tough couple of weeks, especially for those pupils who had been at the school for three years or more. As usual at these challenging times, staff put in the extra time, effort and the innovative thinking required. One particular pupil could only be made to feel more secure if he had a weekly meeting with the building manager and daily guided tours round the new building (while it was being built). The questions he had were endless, and while this could be placed in his own model of human nature and autism, for staff, it was just Jonathon being Jonathon. For a few months, it was accepted that Jonathon would talk about the new building with staff at lunchtimes. Nobody in authority knew what the bell would sound like in our new school. To Jonathon, this was of vital importance because of the structure this sound would give to the day, and for reasons of fire and safety drills. Whereas Jonathon was clearly anxious, Billy did not have any concerns about this huge move. Jonathon and Billy have wildly differing models. To ease the transition into our new school, we wrote to the buildings manager to ask if our pupils could have a look round. All of the pupils looked forward to this. We donned our yellow fluorescent jackets and hard hats and had a tour of the building site. Pupils were shown where the new resource base would be. For Billy, it was enough. For Jonathon, it merely created a whole new set of questions.

There is no set model for autism or ASDs. Matthew is a brilliant 15-year-old Y10 pupil. He has received some counselling about Asperger's Syndrome and initially found it all quite distressing. He disagreed vehemently about the challenges within the area of creative thinking that someone with AS might have. Matthew, when faced with a whiteboard full of scientific methodology, will spend great swathes of time replacing the boring words with ones that demonstrate a little more imagination and creativity. He will do the same in Food Technology, one of his favourite lessons. In English lessons and assignments, this creativity is a big plus for Matthew and we feel he has the potential to follow the subject at A Level. In Science, Matthew asserts 'control' by using his creative skills in language. Science interests Matthew much less than English, History and Food. He is massively creative. He is 'rigidly creative'. Matthew has his own (I suspect) unique model.

This is your mission (should you choose to accept it): write a specific target that is attainable, measurable and recordable to prevent Matthew being so creative in Science. We do need him to spend less time being creative in Science and more time being 'scientific'. He needs to find more ways to exert control over his environment that is for sure. I have faith that this exertion of appropriate control will come largely with the natural maturation process, given that he continues to receive appropriate guidance and support. That continued and appropriate guidance and support is the key for Matthew. In the meantime, all staff can do is encourage and praise Matthew in his creative lessons, and explain honestly and reasonably why sometimes, accurate copying of scientific word equations might be quite important, at least for the next (and probably last) eighteen months of his scientific academic school life anyway. The relationships staff build with pupils like Matthew are the foundation of these difficult and often painful discussions.

Matthew would like to be a published author as an adult. His great heroes are Roald Dahl, The Rev. W. Awdry and Jacqueline Wilson. This is the first few paragraphs from one of several books he is working on at the moment:

> Having been staying in Reidfield since 1939 as a troubled and virtually unloved evacuee, I had fully recovered from the effects of the Second World War by this time and was now a budding railway enthusiast. One Saturday afternoon in March 1957, I remember sitting on the embankment of the deep cutting between Graenery Green and Little Reidfield Tunnel looking over the various train numbers I had managed to jot down while at the same time standing on the platform bench to get a better view of my surroundings. Standing on a bench was compulsory due to the crowds of school children that flooded station platforms these days.

> I'd only just reached a very important number (which just happened to be 60103 – the Flying Scotsman) when the sound of a whistle that I'd been waiting for reached my ears and I

promptly rose to my feet. The whistle sounded again, a good deal louder this time, and before long the train pulled into view. It was probably the most handsome, if down to earth train that I'd ever seen in Reidfield. The locomotive was a six-wheeled War Department Austerity Saddletank wearing a rather tatty olive green livery. The coaches that followed were wearing the same uncared for livery of maroon, smattered with dirt.

I'd completed the jotting of numbers by this time and before long I found myself passing Kilt's farm, waving briefly to Farmer Henry Highlander, a tall, ginger haired, rather good-looking young man with a bony, soldier's face. He beamed delightedly (for I was actually quite popular with the locals in that area) and even his wife Victoria, a rather stout, rosy-faced woman, managed a pleasant smile. I carried on until I reached Reidfield village centre. It was rather large for a village with rows of shops in the very centre. At one end of this row was the post office where Leonard Birmingham, a pale-faced, strong-limbed postman, was delivering the latest letters from the nearby railway station, to Miss Isabel Golspie, an elderly, silver-haired, amazingly beautiful woman who acted as the local postmistress. There was a large Edwardian building which housed a fishmonger's shop owned by Alfred Fowey, a man with a clean-cut, swashbuckling face and hair that reminded you of flowing water, and his wife Judy, a woman with similar hair but a subtle, if proud appearance...

Now, have you accepted your mission as a neurotypical and written Matthew's targets for science lessons?

There was certainly no model of development, success criteria or agreed approaches eleven years ago when The Resource took camp in this bustling secondary school. The staff and pupils were not consulted about our arrival. It was a predominantly white, middle-class school and some of the teachers were understandably fearful about what we were going to do in their lessons. It had a new Head Teacher who like most of his staff, was starting his autism learning curve from very close to zero. I had always worked in wonderful special schools up until this point. From what I saw in lessons Shaun and Andrew, the first two pupils, were going to be scared, confused and wanting to flee back to the safety of the lovely special school from which they had transferred at the age of 11. When I walked into meetings after school, people went quiet. They had no idea who I was or why I was wandering into their lives. Worse than that, I had little idea what I wanted for Shaun and Andrew or why I was there. I wanted to run back to the safety of the lovely special school I had taught at for the previous five years.

Looking back, I tried to have no preconceived ideas about what might work and what might fail. That was impossible to achieve because however open minded you are, your own hang-ups from school follow closely wherever you go. I had not stepped into a mainstream secondary school since I was a pupil myself in the 1970s. I hated and despised Modern Foreign Languages at school mainly because I was literally, useless at French. It was impossible for me to imagine Shaun and Andrew spending two hours a week in French lessons. Then to pick up German in their second year – no chance. They were both experiencing enough challenges interpreting English. I could use these couple of hours each week doing other more useful work, like teaching road safety because the school was split into two buildings with a road in between. Hardly the most convenient arrangement, especially as the teachers stayed in their classrooms while the pupils (and me) moved between the two buildings. This is great in the summer, but not pleasant in an English winter. I discussed my feelings about French lessons with Shaun and Andrew and was firmly put in my place. Shaun felt it was important to try everything because he did not know what he would like or dislike. Andrew felt that French might be, 'a bit of a laugh'. My laughter could be heard from some miles away. Shaun was bemused and scared by this huge secondary school with 1200 pupils. However, he was not going to miss out on anything. They both dragged me kicking and screaming into French lessons and we actually had a good time. Our French teacher, an Austrian woman new to the school and from the sounds of her accent, fairly new to the country, was lovely. The structured style of the teacher and the fact that Andrew and Shaun were starting from a similar level of ability to all their peers meant that I had little to do other than enjoy learning French myself. I met her in a pub recently and she told me that she was so scared by everything, that Andrew and Shaun caused her no extra undue anxieties.

Some of the pupils now opt to drop their Modern Foreign Language after a few years. However, some pupils pass GCSEs in French and it has been known for a couple of pupils to get a C grade or above. One girl who came to us as close to a self-elective mute, got a D grade in French recently. I am constantly amazed by children on the spectrum of all abilities. Kevin is a 15-year-old Y10 pupil who by hard work and determination has ended up in top set French. Kevin has the misfortune to be supported by me in one of his French lessons each week. The pace in this top set is too much for me, and sometimes for Kevin, but it does feel good when we both succeed in keeping up with the other bright sparks.

If there is any kind of philosophy or model which remains today from this early teaching from Shaun and Andrew it is this: if staff can remain open to the pupils, willing to learn from them, spend time listening rather than talking, be willing to facilitate their ideas, and aim for their dreams, then even the most apparently hostile environment like a secondary school can become autism friendly.

This is never an easy approach for people to see at first hand. It takes time and is based on the building of close and trusting relationships. Kevin and I get on well. At the end of the day, as he walks to get onto his minibus, Kevin likes to have a little 'rough and tumble' with me. He kind of charges and bumps into me. There is a problem with this. He is twice the size of me. If I am not looking, I literally get killed in the stampede. There have been times when he has pushed me towards his minibus, and I am sure that if Kevin could have his own way, he would push me into the bus and we would go home together.

Last year Kevin needed an operation on both of his legs because his walking on tiptoes was becoming a real problem. His wonderful mother took Kevin to the hospital on the appointed day. Before the operation Kevin was not allowed to eat (a major challenge) and they had to wait a long time before being taken onto the ward. When they finally got into the anaesthetics room, Kevin would not have the cannula needed in order to fix a line into the back of his hand. Two surgeons, his mother, an anaesthetist and three nurses could not hold Kevin down. They left without the operation being performed.

I was fortunate to be able to speak to Kevin's surgeon the next day and we discussed the problems and how they could be overcome. He has my gratitude, simply for talking to me in the first place, and for trying to understand Kevin's fears and anxieties. We agreed that Kevin needed to be taken straight onto the ward on arrival (early in the morning) and given a large dose of 'knockout' medicine so that he would be nice and relaxed (for relaxed, read high) before going into the anaesthetics room. He also allowed me to go with Kevin and his mum right up to the bit where he would disappear into the operating theatre. We talked this through with Kevin and he agreed to give it another go. We arrived, and a wonderful nurse managed to get Kevin to take the knockout medicine by shooting it into his throat with a syringe, and then we wheeled him into the anaesthetics room. Some administrative worker who had not been warned did mumble something about the fact that we should not be in this 'hallowed room', but the surgeon waved her protestations away. It was like a scene from a TV hospital drama. Kevin was so spaced out by this time, he did not care whether the cannula went in his hand or his left ear. Life had become a series of colourful, soft images for spaced-out Kevin. He emerged several hours later wanting to hug Mum, me and anyone else close at hand. He was rightly proud of himself. I had been there. The rest of the team covered my roles for that day. I often wonder what the LEA would have made of that. Perhaps I should have taken the day as unpaid leave. There is probably a form I should have filled in. Kevin and I are now the equivalent of war buddies. The spin-offs have been enormous. Kevin now wants to succeed at school, has become more organised and increasingly sociable. His attitude is very much that nothing can be as hard as going through that operation and the four months' recovery period.

I could match that example for each member of staff working in different settings with a variety of pupils. There is no model for this, no tick chart and no recordable evidence. Visitors will see pupils who are doing OK. They might see Kevin move to sit near me at dinnertime with a pack of cards and a bag of plastic money. He likes to gamble at cards and make up his own games so that he wins. However, I have managed to teach him two card games that are not dependent on gambling. If there was a sheet of previous traumas, conflicts and compromises reached to show to the visitor at that point, I would hand it over. There is no need.

They may see another pupil talking with friends over lunch. What they fail to see is how angry he used to be with me and other staff because we were not getting it right for him. Initially, staff would sell their souls to the devil to make it right for this lad. To a non-anorak, this might have seemed like giving in to his demands. From doing no homework at home, this lad has just handed in a detailed and lengthy History project on the Romans. I wish there was a tick chart to show this progress. I wish there had been a model that we could have followed. However, there are no short cuts. He did not believe we were on his side. Now he does. He did not like us, now he thinks we are kind of all right. He could not organise his bag because of having books, lunchbox and PE kit. The first time he could not do this his world fell apart and boy, did we know about it. After discussing it, we decided that he would ask me to pack his bag after lunch if he could not do it. I do not mind doing this. I have a strong suspicion that he will be able to sort this challenge out himself in a few years' time. Perhaps it should be one of his aims or targets. But maybe we should just be brave enough to think that if things are 'right', pupils will make progress at their own pace. We have to be patient and look at all possible avenues to reduce anxieties so that this progress can occur naturally. There is no timescale to this, nor is it rocket science. When teaching and guidance are needed alongside, staff are there with resources, explanations and the time to answer questions and allay fears.

Perhaps as human beings, we ought to spend the maximum amount of time possible building relationships, trust and understanding. This is not as easy as it sounds in a busy secondary school with all the demands made by the curriculum and a staff that, like many others in the teaching profession, are suffering from 'initiative overload'. Sometimes the best things happen when we just sit and chat with a pupil. The most fragile of lesson plans and schemes of work can turn into those magical times when you actually feel as if you are making progress.

One 12-year-old Y7 pupil decided he did not want to go to music lessons any more because they were 'rubbish'. Fortunately, I was in

The Resource on a non-contact period for this hour each week. Staff felt that this pupil needed to examine his Asperger's Syndrome more closely, something he had been reluctant to do in the past. We sat and read a bit of Luke Jackson's book *Freaks, Geeks and Asperger Syndrome*. We got into a discussion about Luke's opinion that Asperger's Syndrome is not a disability, but a gift. The hour sped by and this pupil talked about the challenges he faces on a daily basis. He talked about how difficult it is for him to know when he has done something wrong. For this reason he needed staff to be honest and clear with him straight away. However, he also discussed the fact that he can over-complicate things because he finds it a challenge to be clear and honest. He had very strong opinions about parents telling their children if they have Asperger's Syndrome and said that he was learning more about it because before he came to secondary school, he did not know many other people on the spectrum. This pupil has a mainstream friend who also went to the same primary school. His friend had said that he was now showing other people that he could behave and that he is smart. Not sure where the tick box is for that one but I look forward to each and every moment of these hour lessons in his company. He is quite happy to teach me about Asperger's Syndrome and I am more than happy to do the majority of the listening.

If I went to a foreign land to stay with a new family, I would hope they would do a lot for me in the early weeks while I was settling in and learning about a new culture and language. I would hope that they might take a lot of responsibilities away from me so that my anxiety levels would not get too high. I could then learn and assimilate without too much adverse pressure. After a while, when I felt more comfortable and trusting, I could begin to take on more responsibility myself. When mistakes were made I could return to the safety of my new family to discuss what went wrong and what my response or course of action could be next time something similar arose. It is easy for me to see that a mistake might not necessarily be followed by calmness, logic and rational thought processes. I hope my new family would want to learn about my culture and language.

We appear to be living in an 'instant' society in some respects. Some people demand things like goods and services in an instant. Answers to problems are sometimes better if they fix something quickly, even if the answer turns out to be only a temporary solution. Guidelines to good practice and proformas to evidence everything and make people accountable, cause more heartache and disappointment to the very people whom they were designed to help. We used to use evidence from a Communication Therapist for Annual Reviews. Communication Therapists, Speech Therapists or whatever title they chose to have are such important professionals. Their services are in short supply. We have had a cracker of a woman coming to see staff and the pupils for the last seven years. Kirsty became part of our team and the pupils loved her very much. She was willing to learn from the pupils and be guided by them about what they wanted to learn. However, much of her time initially was spent in doing assessments and obtaining 'scores' that we could use in the Annual Review fifteen-page documentation. We were hoping to show that some communication skills for most of our pupils were improving. We wanted to provide evidence, be accountable and show that what we were doing was making a difference. Over a period of time, this evidence could be used to help the LEA decide which pupils might do best by coming to our provision, and which ones may need a more intensive approach within a special school. We are lucky in Sheffield to have some excellent special schools that do great work with children and teenagers on the spectrum.

Annual Reviews were dutifully sent off to the LEA with Kirsty's report attached including lists of assessment scores. Comparing these scores (e.g. sentence formation, comprehension, sequencing and use of social language, etc.) with baseline results, Kirsty and the staff were delighted to see good improvements in a majority of pupils over two or three years. Some pupils in some of these tests were coming out with scores that placed them within the 'normal range', whatever that is. Sadly, a different kind of computer generated letter started arriving from the LEA. It went something like this:

> Pupil A is doing well. We can see that from his academic progress and from the improvement in his scores as demonstrated by the Communication Therapist. A discussion needs to occur before Pupil A's next Annual Review about the transfer into his/her local mainstream secondary school.

This happened for four pupils one year. We had provided an 'instant fix' for a life long disability. These four pupils were doing extremely well. Moving them could have worked, but you and I know it could have been a grave error. They were doing well because they were happy and settled. They could rely on having adults to turn to when issues arose. They knew that any issues would be dealt with appropriately and to their satisfaction. They knew we were on their side. Sometimes I am criticised for being too idealistic. In this case, I was a practitioner. The LEA were the idealists. Several phone calls later, the LEA corrected the misunderstanding and it has not risen again. Since then, we agreed with Kirsty that the best approach would be to stop doing assessments with pupils. Nobody can see the progress our pupils are making because our only reliable source of assessment is no longer used. The next table should be evidence from our Communication Therapist about the (sometimes) remarkable progress the majority of our pupils are making. But, it does not exist so you will just have to imagine it. It would have been good, but then so is your imagination.

One of these 'wonder pupils' had his fourteenth birthday at a similar time to the LEA's computer splurging out these coded letters of congratulation. As an 11- or 12-year-old Y7 pupil he had got into several 'scrapes' because he saw no need to conceal his intelligence. Other pupils saw him as arrogant and confrontational. The lad had made good progress socially over a couple of years. He brought me in his party invitations because he wanted me to check them out. There was to be a get-together at his house. His invitations were those mass produced ones where you only have to fill in the necessary gaps. However, on the back he had written, 'If you can't think of a present to buy me, don't worry, just bring the cash'. A subtle mistake to explain to this lad, but what could have been a glaring error for his mainstream peers if these invitations had been sent out. As Margaret Dewey says (in Frith 1991), 'In this sense, an autistic person can be blind to the meaning of a situation. No helper of the blind would react with ridicule, anger or fear to a request for visual help.' (p.201). In another school, without the necessary backup or close relationships, maybe this lad would not have even been thinking about having a party to celebrate his birthday in the first place. His error, led to more teaching and a greater understanding. What his mainstream peers learn naturally, this lad, however academically able, still needs to be taught scientifically.

It takes a strong and cohesive team of people to work without models, formulas or agreed guidelines. Some people like to make things up as they go along, and others find that approach extremely stressful. The turnover of staff at The Resource has been low over the eleven years. Our sickness record has been equally low. Sociologists point to an optimum size of seven or eight people in a group for a team to function at its most cohesive. A larger team than this size might develop into two or three smaller groups. This can have its benefits and its challenges. Our team of two teachers, and almost nine Specialist Support Workers are roughly split into 'two camps'. However, this is a model of our choosing. Some staff like to work alongside lower school pupils (aged from 11 to 14 years old) and others like to work with upper school pupils (aged from 14 to 16 years old). I make a willing attempt to 'manage' the upper school team and my colleague Lucy, as the second teacher, manages the lower school team. There is always a little overlap. I do look forward to a lower set Maths lesson with Y8 pupils last thing on a Friday afternoon – honest.

The successful member of staff in The Resource will be someone who is calm, yet lively, patient, full of ingenuity and humour, honest with themselves, and able to handle bucketfuls of stress. It is not a job for someone who is easily depressed, or someone who brings their issues to work with them. At the expense of sounding arrogant, I believe a degree of charisma is also very important. I am blessed to be surrounded by a team of charismatic, honest, patient and well-balanced people. They make my life easy. Children look forward to coming to school largely because of the people in this special team. Claire Sainsbury (2000) states that there are some key characteristics needed by a teacher of children with Asperger's Syndrome. These include: being attracted to differences and the unknown, the ability to give without getting an ordinary thank you and a willingness to adapt one's natural style of communication and social interaction. She concludes by saying that the best teachers 'also seem to have a genuine enjoyment and appreciation of the quirks of children with AS' (p.99).

When we have a post advertised, the demand to work at the school with pupils on the autistic spectrum is usually high. However, I sometimes think that the job description sent out does put a lot of people off. I could write here again about the disgusting levels of pay that our LEAs pay Specialist Support staff in their schools, but I have already made that point. It is worth putting people off from applying for jobs working with people on the spectrum and a specific, demanding and lengthy job description can help with this just as much as low levels of financial reward. People have to have a strong desire to work at The Resource. I guess I am looking for anoraks or potential anoraks. The job description and details are given below.

Background

The Governors wish to appoint a Special Secondary Assistant to work in The Resource. The Resource caters for pupils who have a Statement of Special Educational Needs that relates to a severe communication disorder, or a severe speech and language disorder. Established in 1994, The Resource is led by Matthew Hesmondhalgh, has one other teacher and nine SSAs. The Resource is also a registered charity. The charity currently employs one member of staff. The Resource has good links with Sheffield College.

The successful candidate will spend around 80 per cent of the timetable supporting one or two pupils in their mainstream lessons. Some time will be spent in The Resource carrying out programmes of learning specifically related to the pupils' needs. There will be a small amount of non-contact time that will be used for preparing work. It is a dedicated and hard-working team of staff in The Resource. King Ecgbert is a demanding and thriving school. The expectations of pupils with severe communication disorders are very high. The Resource, its staff and the work they carry out is held in high regard. This post has much to offer the successful candidate.

King Ecgbert is currently a split-site school and this post does have some physical demands. Staff are expected to walk between buildings (which takes about six minutes), support in PE lessons and go on some residential activities. The Resource base is located in the Wessex building and has a good view of the very pleasant countryside and playing fields!

Person specification

Essential

- suitable qualifications/experience as an SSA or something similar/equivalent
- to like children, especially those with additional needs and have high expectations of them
- excellent interpersonal skills
- the ability to work as part of a team
- to be reliable, have the ability to work hard and give freely of your time
- flexibility of thought and good problem solving skills
- the ability to use initiative
- the ability to learn from others
- good organisational skills.

Desirable

- to have participated, or be interested in extra curricular activities
- to have an interest or expertise in ICT
- a good sense of humour
- particular skills within the curriculum
- some knowledge or experience of autism
- experience at secondary level, i.e. Key Stages 3 and 4.

Applications

Complete the application form which should be hand written. Make sure you supply us with the telephone/fax number of your referees and your current place of employment (if appropriate) so that we can contact them.

Include a letter of application which should be *word-processed* and no more than two sides of A4 containing the following:

- how you feel that your experiences and/or qualifications relate to the person specification
- why you have applied for this post
- what you have to offer King Ecgbert School and The Resource in particular
- why you want to work with pupils with severe communication disorders.

Good luck

Matthew Hesmondhalgh

I think this job description and specification puts a lot of people off from applying for a post at The Resource. Brilliant. Of the ten to fifteen people who do eventually apply, three or four tend to be interesting characters who deserve to go through the gruelling experience of an interview with our Head Teacher (and me). For as long as I can remember, we also have one of the Specialist Support Workers sitting in on interviews as an observer. This is not permitted by our Head Teacher for any other department in school.

The most disappointing people at interview are undoubtedly the ones who come with great swathes of experience in the field, but a stack of pre-conceived ideas. They have their models and answers already worked out. I think personnel issues are among the most difficult but I would have a tendency to steer clear of this kind of candidate. In practice, our interviews are scripted to make it fair. They should be scored according to a list of criteria as judged against the job specification. In reality, my Head Teacher likes to veer away from the agreed script, sometimes at tangents I am hard pressed to understand. He will often ask, 'what three things would you take on a desert island?' He really enjoys interviewing people and in time, this has relaxed what I find quite a stressful process.

The interviews are never scored. People who work in human resources would probably find this hard to imagine. Between the three of us, we usually pick the most open, honest, quick-witted and thoughtful people. The successful person may have no secondary experience, or no experience with people on the spectrum. They are usually people looking for a fresh challenge. The Head and I have disagreed twice over people at interview. On both occasions, his word was final, and he was right. If you are interested, unless one of the three 'things' you would take on a desert island is a person, you may not get the job. Fit that one into a model or guideline.

The current team is as strong as ever. If I am not doing my job well there are well meaning people in the team quick to point it out. There are many issues that pull us together. Shared experiences count for a lot. Our conferences and training sessions are days when everyone works to the same goals. People in the team are supportive and caring towards each other. We socialise together. One of my favourite nights out was when (a predominantly female staff team) wore tinsel halos and badges declaring themselves 'Matthew's Angels'. I had to wear the devil's horns and carry a pitchfork. I am privileged to work along-side brilliant, innovative and caring people.

So, are you convinced yet that the Triad of Impairments needs to be confined to the past? Can you dare to cope without it in your work or parenting? Do you still need this out-dated and simplistic crutch? Think about your son or daughter, or some of the children with whom you work. Get a large piece of paper, draw a model for them and then think of a name for it. File it under 'interesting but not that relevant'. Do the same for yourself. It is good 'therapy' if nothing else. Then get back to what needs to be the major part of our job: talking to other neurotypicals about the strengths (and needs) of individuals who have not yet been confident or at ease enough to show their best skills. Pupils from The Resource, students from Sheffield College and those young adults in paid employment, are certainly ready for society and the 'outside world'. I am not yet convinced that society is anywhere near ready enough for the young people I am privileged to work alongside. Of all the 'models' of society eulogised about over the past 2,000 years, there is not one that has seen people with ASDs at their best. If we are to judge a society by how it treats the most disadvantaged people in it, then we need to examine (and change) society much more intensely than look for models to help us 'explain' autism.

CHAPTER 3

How Does a Service Become Autism Specific?

This is usually one of the central themes in the majority of questions asked by visitors to The Resource, or at conferences. By now the reader should realise that I am not going to magically produce a lovely model, or action plan that can be followed in order for a service to become autism friendly. People in the field have to deal with neurotypicals within a wider context of work, families, management structures, a lack of common sense and general incompetence. These other pushes and pulls have to be understood if we are to make positive changes for people on the spectrum. The flip side of that same coin is that good attempts have to be made to try to understand and empathise with the individual on the spectrum. A famous football manager in England once said that his team's success was due to 1 per cent inspiration and 99 per cent perspiration. This is true when working with people on the spectrum, in any institution. A degree of luck is also needed, as any honest football manager will tell you.

Shaun left The Resource after five years to do a course at college in Health and Social Care. He took pride in his C grade in English Literature and his D grades in History and Maths. His love of history, people and life were all still intact as he left school, all achievements to be proud of. His course option at college was largely based on a successful weekly work placement at an elderly people's day care centre during his final year at school. Shaun had decided that his future lay in working with the elderly.

When I phoned the manager of a nearby elderly people's home, I fully expected to have my request politely refused. Instead, the manager of the centre became very excited by Shaun's planned placement (there's our bit of luck). She told me that his placement would be great for 'inter-generational relationships'. I just nodded politely and as usual, tried to appear wiser by saying nothing. As Shaun and myself were about to enter the day care centre for the first time, he asked me what he should talk about with the elderly people. Under pressure, I replied that he should talk about anything that interested him. Shaun quite clearly related old people to his love of all things historical. We entered his new work place. He sat next to an elderly man who must have been at least eighty. In a voice that was typically Shaun's (full blast) he asked this man what role he had played in the Second World War. Without skipping a beat, the man replied that he had been an engineer on the submarines. Shaun's face lit up. For the next twenty minutes, this wonderful elderly man and this equally wonderful young man talked about the Second World War. They also discussed Shaun's schooling, which greatly interested the older man. Questions flowed back and forth. I sat in the corner, quietly drinking my hot chocolate and watched inter-generational relationships happening before my very eyes.

Shaun has a hearing impairment in one ear. This probably explains his louder voice in some situations. Without wanting to generalise or be disrespectful, a larger proportion of elderly people do experience challenges in the hearing department. Shaun and elderly people became a match made in heaven. Shaun became the bingo caller on his weekly placement at the day care centre. If there was a quiz, Shaun was the quizmaster. Both Shaun and I joined in with the armchair aerobics.

After one year at college of his Health and Social Care course, Shaun decided that a job within the caring professions was not for him. He wanted a job in an office. I (honestly!) cherish these moments when a teenager just decides to change direction completely. The husband of a colleague spotted a Modern Apprenticeship in Office and Administration run by Sheffield City Council and their housing department. This course involved four days' paid employment within a busy council housing department and one day at college to gain a

Level Two GNVQ in Office and Administration. If successful on the two-year course, a job would be guaranteed.

Shaun applied and I managed to speak to one of the people involved with the course. He also happened to be on the interview panel. He kindly agreed to allow me to sit in on Shaun's interview. Over twenty young people were to be interviewed for seven vacancies on the course. It was made clear before Shaun's interview that he would find it challenging to cope with members of the public in stressful situations. The interviews were in my summer holiday which was lucky, although there was little I could do to prepare Shaun for the interview. Shaun arrived to meet me and as usual, looked more smartly dressed than me. The questions were tough. For example, 'What is the role of a council?' Shaun found it difficult and I did not hold out a lot of hope. After his interview, the two men on the panel both commented that Shaun had given better answers than most. They listened to me waffle on about Shaun and his strengths. They did not feel it would present too many difficulties if Shaun could not manage a 'front line' post, and Shaun was awarded a place on the course.

For the two years of the course, Shaun received almost full support from our Employment Support Worker. This is a person employed by our charity. Shaun worked for four days a week in an open plan office along with about sixty to seventy other people. His desk was next to a window on the third floor of a building in town. The phones rang constantly. I could never work out how anyone could concentrate in this atmosphere. Shaun loved each and every day. He gradually extended the number of administrative tasks he could do. One job was to check, record and distribute the incoming mail. Another job was to add up the weekly hours worked by his colleagues to the nearest fifteen minutes so that their wages could be accurately calculated. With support, Shaun gradually learnt about the workings of a busy office. One day he was awarded with a certificate for being employee of the month. He loved his co-workers and they loved him. In preparation for his exams, Shaun came back to The Resource a few times to revise. After his two years were successfully completed, Shaun got a job and his employer rightly kept him in the same department doing the same jobs. For the following year, Shaun received three days a week support from our Employment Support Worker. During his fourth year, Shaun received 1.5 days a week support from us. Only now, four years after starting have we decided that Shaun can manage on his own. There is no time scale to providing an autism specific service. There is no room for failure. Shaun needed support for a long time if he was to be successful in his job. There is a financial cost to providing this support. However, if the support had not been provided, Shaun could now easily be sat at home doing very little. There is now enough support and understanding within the office towards Shaun. His co-workers have started their learning curve through necessity. Our financial investment over the four years (note the word investment – *not* cost) was in the region of £30,000. Shaun is now a useful and valued employee who can successfully complete a wide variety of tasks. Was the investment worth it? Of course.

For me there is no choice. Investment in our friends like Shaun should never be questioned. If this investment is not yet funded through the statutory agencies, then the voluntary/charitable sector has to step in. This is one central theme of why I feel that work and progress within the field of ASDs is now in danger of stagnating. Charities have had no choice but to step in and fill the void in too many situations. The statutory sector will gladly let this happen. This leaves all involved having to fund valuable projects and at the same time, shout about the injustices that allow situations like this to continue and multiply. The problem-solving skills Shaun had to apply at school, college and now in full-time employment are far beyond those that most 'regular' people have to even consider. The problem-solving skills that politicians need to apply to situations like this are basic in comparison.

When I walked into King Ecgbert School eleven years ago, the Head Teacher gave me a cupboard to work from. I love to hear stories of new resource bases that have opened around the UK in the last eleven years because they appear to have learnt from our mistakes. They have working parties, time and budgets to make sure the provision is right for everyone. Being autism specific or autism friendly has to start with as much consultation and planning as possible. Any doubts about a provision must be answered as honestly as possible by the right people (not usually someone from the LEA). The Governors of a nearby mainstream primary school recently refused to have a small resource for pupils with ASDs. Some of them visited our resource and the brilliant Head Teacher of the primary school came as well. However, the initial approaches and public meetings about the proposal were lead by people from the LEA. It would have been nice to be invited to some of those vital initial consultation meetings. After all, this primary resource would have fed into our provision at King Ecgbert School. This raising of consciousness is important if people are going to feel empowered to put forward suggestions and ideas. I recently visited a lovely secondary school in York that was in the process of planning a resource base for pupils on the spectrum. The Head, Deputy, SENCO and representatives from the LEA, were all discussing the arrangements for the new resource base. They were positive, knowledgeable and full of ideas. The questions they asked were relevant, honest and searching. I hope my responses were in the same style. I am certain the provision in their secondary school will be first class. When I stepped out of my cupboard eleven years ago, it was by myself and with so much fear and trepidation, that I did not stay out for long.

I think that we scare ourselves silly trying to be autism specific without actually thinking about what it means. To be honest, I am not sure what it means exactly and it seems to differ slightly from day to day depending on the situation and person to whom I am talking. I do know it is a vital area. However, I also feel strongly that sometimes, professionals can be a little precious about the term, especially those who lack recent hands-on experience. We have built being 'autism specific' into something magical and wonderful and I am not sure that it is either of these things.

In Y8, when pupils are aged from 12 to 13 years old, in our school there is a half-week residential trip into the beautiful countryside of Derbyshire. Over the years, all but one of the pupils we have worked with have gone on this residential trip. The pupils are away from home for two nights and three days. This trip is an important social time and a chance for new friendships to be forged. Mainstream teachers can stop being teachers and actually have time to enjoy the company of teenagers. There are organised outdoor activities and social events in the evening.

Daniel had never been away from home before and was adamant he would not go on the Y8 residential trip. Staff talked to Daniel and his mum (who was keen for her son to go). Other pupils who had been on the trip in previous years talked to Daniel about the great time they had. Daniel agreed to go and visit the place where he and his peers would be staying. The manager of the residential provision was very accommodating. Daniel, and his friend Jonathon from The Resource (who had no problems with going) were able to see where they would sleep, eat and play. Daniel wanted a second visit to check it out even further, and this was arranged. He bravely decided to give it a go. No direct pressure was applied at school or home. These two visits helped Daniel to see that the place was all right, and not too far from home. Daniel knew that a member of staff from The Resource would be going on the trip. They would be there for him at all times, day or night. Then a problem arose. Staff in The Resource felt that Daniel and his friend Jonathon would need to have a separate bedroom. This would satisfy their need for peace, calm, low sensory factors and a decent night's sleep. This was not possible due to lack of space and they would have to share a room with three other lads from their form. This is one of the many occasions when we have to hold our hands up and say, 'we got it wrong'. These three other lads took pleasure from sharing a room with Daniel and Jonathon. They learnt more about Daniel and Jonathon, and vice versa. I went out on the first morning with some trepidation, to have breakfast with Daniel, Jonathon and my colleague. Everything was fine. The whole trip went well, Daniel was suitably proud of himself and he basked in the praise of staff and parents alike. I phoned Daniel's dad during his first night back at home. His dad was desperate to hear about the trip and what his son had been doing. However, Daniel was exhausted from the physical activity and the sensory overload. He was having some 'quiet time' in his bedroom. Dad knew to leave Daniel alone and that there would be other times to catch up with his son.

One of my other Y8 friends was due to go on a similar trip to Daniel and Jonathon's, but at a different time in the year. She is an academically gifted top set pupil who is slowly exploring our world and sometimes struggles to cope with many things such as noise, movement and the social rules by which most of us try to abide. She loses her temper because of her Asperger's Syndrome, not because she has challenging behaviour. This girl was desperate to go on the residential trip. Staff were not so sure. The risks involved certainly had to be minimised as much as possible. It would have been impossible for her to share with other girls from her form. The noise of giggling would have been too distressing. My friend likes a lot of quiet time even though she is improving her tolerance levels of others. We decided to send two members of staff on this particular trip, however it was not appropriate for the girl to share a bedroom with the two staff members. There were about sixty other pupils going on the trip and there was literally no room at the inn. We put in another call to the lovely, understanding manager of the centre, explaining the situation and expressing our feelings that this experience could be a positive one, and might even provide some breakthroughs for this young girl. He was brilliant again, and we were lucky. The residential provision next door to the one our school was to use, just happened to be vacant for the necessary three days. He arranged for two bedrooms to be available in this adjacent building at no extra cost (not that a financial cost would have stopped us at this point). My friend could join in with the activities, mealtimes and social times, and yet retreat to the sanctuary of her bedroom if necessary. She had a brilliant time and loved every minute of this valuable experience. I am indebted to those staff that volunteer to go on these residential trips, both specialist and mainstream. We live in times when such trips are under threat because of the 'accident and sue them' culture. Risks do need to be assessed and minimised, but they can never be reduced to zero. For trips such as these to disappear because teachers (understandably) will not take on the small risks involved would be a great shame. Parents can have a few nights off. Their sons and daughters will remember the trip away to Derbyshire for ever.

If these are examples of good autism practice, or they highlight issues that need to be addressed if a service is to become autism specific, then I will hold my hand up and take credit for them. I think that the Head Teacher of our school may be nearer the mark when he describes our approaches as ones based on common sense, a good knowledge of the pupils with whom we work and a sheer bloody stubbornness to stand up for the children and fight for their rights. The application of common sense and standing up for the rights of children is never easy in a busy secondary school. Common sense is not always that common.

If parents of children with ASDs are the two-fisted street fighters of the disability movement, then the professionals have to be the hired sharp shooters standing by their side. There is always going to be the next fight, the next challenge or the next adventure. If we are to be 'friendly' or 'specific' to people on the spectrum, we have to take up these challenges however uncomfortable or complex they might be. The next generation of parents, professionals and anoraks must not be able to criticise us for ignoring these challenges. People in future generations will probably look back at our methods, philosophies and ideas with, at best, some confusion. We look back on some of the theories of the 1970s and 1980s with disbelief. For example, what was Forced Holding Therapy all about? This practice of, for example, holding a child's head to force eye contact must have resulted in untold damage. I would share Claire Sainsbury's view that this was a form of sensory rape. However, what we must not allow is for future generations of parents and professionals to see that we ducked out of battles when we should have stood up to be counted. That would be unforgivable. A few of my fellow professionals around the UK criticise my 'confrontational' style and language. That is their problem. Not too many of them are engaged in daily contact with people on the spectrum anyway, so their ideas and views can easily become out-dated. I will happily concede that there is a vital role for academics to play within the field of autism. Universities provide great debating houses. Research is vital in any field. However, I also feel that we put our top academics on somewhat of a pedestal. We look to the academics and theorists to provide a lead, and influence our future practice. That role can only be played by people with ASDs themselves, parents and workers in frontline services. Philosophers have attempted to interpret the world around them for centuries. I guess that leaves the rest of us free to try and change it for the better.

Trying to consider the human qualities involved in being autism specific is a bit like trying to nail jelly to a wall. For most anoraks, I think there is something instinctive about this way of being. However, that adds to some idea of mystery. It also runs the risk of appearing 'saint like' and arrogant. Yet, I have known staff in The Resource be totally focused on the person with an ASD with whom they are working, and I have known staff who just do not find that 'groove'. A teacher at my first school in the mid-1980s solved the distress or tantrums of one pupil by placing a ruler on his desk. I could only guess at the threat that this ruler carried. A pupil who chewed his pencil was served the offending item for dinner. There were other punitive methods used which are too distressing to mention. There was nothing autism friendly about it. I resigned after one year (with no job to go to).

Sometimes, The Resource will take a child whose distress at something can turn into threatening or challenging behaviour. The step up to a mainstream secondary school (even with support) is a huge one and should never be underestimated. The first term can pose challenges for new pupils and staff alike, all of whom face a steep learning curve. A higher number of mistakes will be made during this first term. The sensory factors in a mainstream secondary school can be over-powering for children with an ASD, and we cannot guarantee to 'get it right' all the time for all pupils. Our pupils have to cope in a neurotypical environment with neurotypical people. The challenging behaviours caused by anxiety or stresses have been greatly alleviated in our new building. The wider corridors, greater natural light and better soundproofing have all helped pupils who experience sensory overload.

Finding yourself with a pupil who is displaying aggressive or challenging behaviour is never easy. Responses differ from pupil to pupil. However, a first 'move' must always be to reduce the size of the audience, noise and movement. The adult must be working at optimum speed and thought to gauge the situation, the possible causes, the safety of others and how best to reach a satisfactory conclusion for all parties. One difficulty is that if faced with a personally harmful situation, the adult must try to be as non-threatening as possible. One way to make yourself less threatening is to drastically reduce the amount of eye contact towards the pupil in distress. At precisely the moment when you want to be seeing everything clearly (especially blows that might be coming your way) staff involved have to mini-mise their eye contact towards the pupil. Negotiation has to take place almost blindfolded. Staff have to be firmly on the side of the pupil at all times. Human beings in distress rarely need to be shouted at (unless they are endangering themselves or others). However, staff have to be able to take this kind of pressure and accept that mistakes will be made that could be potentially harmful to themselves. If a pupil raises a chair over the head of a member of staff and threatens in anger to bring it crashing down, it does take a certain something to decide:

1. I'm not going to look directly at this pupil or the chair.

2. I'm going to stay calm.

3. I'm 95 per cent certain that this chair is not going to come crashing down on my head, and that is good enough.

4. We will negotiate a solution that is acceptable to me and the distressed pupil, because if we don't, a similar situation will probably arise again.

5. I am going to need a witness who will watch this situation without intervening, just in case it goes wrong.

These are the key moments when real and lasting friendships are forged. Think of your best friend and ask yourself why they are such a special person? It could be because you have both shared special experiences. Special experiences can be tough times just as easily as nice, happy times. One of my friends who did not bring the chair crashing down on top of my head told me a funny joke at the end of the day as we were waiting for her minibus to arrive. She whispered in my ear 'Mr Matthew, if quizzes are quizzical, then what are tests?' The member of staff with her said that she was a little worried about telling me the joke because of its rudeness. I loved it.

This kind of philosophy or attempts at being autism friendly is nothing new in educational terms. In his book, *Freedom To Learn* (1983), Carl Rogers talks about a company of people emerging from within a climate of 'unconditional positive regard and respect, empathy and personal genuineness' (p.174). I think that for seven hours a day, five days a week, forty weeks a year, the team of staff at The Resource have to put aside all their human frailties as neurotypicals. They have to negotiate deals and keep promises, listen at length to words they have heard before, be prepared to sell their mother if one pupil shows any sign of making a small step forward, say what they mean and mean what they say and be prepared not to take anything personally. They have to have empathic waves gushing out of every pore. When I return home from this superhuman effort, my daughters should know to place no demands on me for about half an hour. It does not always work out that way. However, I guess many parents of children on the spectrum would sell their soul for a five-day week and a forty-week year.

The staff, alongside me, will make mistakes on a regular basis. This is because we are neurotypicals. I do not 'buy into' the argument that we are all somewhere on the spectrum. That would be like saying we all have a hearing impairment or are partially sighted. Neurotypicals have no right to somehow take away, or belittle the disability of autism. I asked one of the most academically able, but sensory impaired children with Asperger's Syndrome at school to write down what he felt like when he walked into mainstream lessons. He wrote: 'Imagine walking on scorching hot sand in bare feet, wearing itchy clothes, through two lines of people screaming at you, in total darkness.' I cannot begin to imagine the anxiety, fear and physical pain he experiences on a daily basis, nor can I measure how much courage some of the pupils are showing just by turning up to school each day. Neurotypicals may be a race of 'curtain straighteners', or 'door shutters'. We may rely on routine to a large extent, but this does not put us all somewhere on the spectrum. Neurotypicals laugh and joke about this area in almost a conspiratorial way and yet I cannot think of another disability where this happens. Nothing can justify trying to steal another's clothes.

Sometimes the National Curriculum just has to be pushed to one side for a period of time. As professionals, we have to be brave enough to do this. Every service I have ever worked in has claimed to be 'child centred'. Our institutions of learning are rarely child centred. They might be 'results centred', 'curriculum centred' or 'financially centred', but the rights of children often have to be pushed aside. Flexibility is an important component of our drive to be autism specific. It is a vital factor in being child centred as well.

When Dave started with us a few years ago, he found life in a secondary school almost intolerable. Even with full support, he disliked the noise levels and the movement around school. He would sit in most lessons and cry quietly. He could not cope with wiping his nose because he did not like the feel of a handkerchief near his face, so he would snort snot onto the desk in front of him. Dave is a good artist, and even using the medium of snot, his spider diagrams were something to treasure.

Staff became better at supporting Dave. He got better at helping staff to support his needs in ways he found comfortable. He developed into a happy pupil with a wicked sense of humour. His second year was great and the start of his third year continued to be smooth. Then a phone call came from his art teacher to say that Dave was in floods of tears (he was independent in this lesson). She had asked the children to draw three pictures, one about their past, one to represent the present and one about their future. When I went to see him, Dave told me (through his tears) that his past was terrible, he was unhappy at the moment and he did not even want to think about his future. We returned to the safety of our resource base and lessons were temporarily abandoned.

Over the next few days, Dave did a lot of artwork to help us understand how he was feeling. This made use of a medium with which he was more than comfortable. His mother and father had separated before he started with us. Dave drew a huge brick wall between himself and his father. He drew his heavily pregnant stepmother towering over a cringing Dave with stars and exclamation marks coming out of her mouth. Dave drew his father cuddling his younger brother (who is not on the spectrum) and telling him that all would be OK. We called Dave's mum in for a chat and she filled in some of the gaps for us. There were some strong feelings expressed towards her ex-husband and his pregnant partner. They had actually got married the previous weekend. Dave and his brother had not been invited. Dave was complaining to his mother that his father loved his younger brother, but that he was expressing anxieties about

Dave's future because of his autism. This negative view of autism did not match with what Dave was discovering about his disability. Dave was not enjoying his weekends with his father. Dave attended this meeting with his mum and talked through what he wanted to happen.

The following day we held a similar meeting with Dave's dad. His pregnant wife came with him. Not the easiest of chats. Dave's dad saw the artwork he had done and was naturally upset by it. We were able to put Dave's suggestions to him and as adults we came up with a few more. Dave's stepmother was told in the nicest possible way to take a back seat for a while. Dave came in during this meeting and was told what would happen in the future on his weekend visits to his dad's house.

I spoke to Dave's father after the first of these weekends. Dave and his dad had made the Sunday dinner. One thing Dave worried about was cooking 'oven meals'. As he said, 'I'm fine at microwave meals 'cause we've done that in The Resource'. Dad bought him some plasticine, which was one of Dave's favourite things to model with. He also bought his son a word search book because Dave said it would help him to 'switch the world off'. Dave's dad is now some-times caught in the middle between the needs of his son and his sec-ond wife. However, Dave's dad and his wife are adults. Dave is a teenager with severe autism. Dave came through this short period of time thinking that the world is a great place and that he actually had some small influence on those adults around him. He happily started lessons again having shaken my hand and saying that it had been a brilliant time with all those meetings.

Dave's work placement is in a trendy skateboarding and kite shop. He quickly became independent for this one afternoon a week and learnt how to use public transport to and from the shop. He has just completed a two-week block of work experience at the shop. I went to visit him one afternoon. As I walked into the shop I could see Dave playing with a yo-yo. I made the mistake of having a joke about the fact that Dave was clearly working very hard. My sarcasm was met with his quick and quiet response, that at that moment in time he was 'on product testing'.

This child-centred approach, as a component of developing an autism specific service is also nothing new. A.S. Neill wrote about his school, Summerhill in the 1960s. Some might see Neill's Summerhill as an 'extreme' example of a child-centred approach; others might use the word 'pure'. Neill saw himself as a 'doer' rather than a great thinker. He wrote, 'we must be on the child's side' (p.114). He talks about having a faith in children and that if you do not have this faith, the child will feel that your love cannot be very deep. He goes on to say, 'When you approve of children you can talk to them about any-thing and everything' (1968, p.114). It is this 'approval' that Carl Rogers calls unconditional positive regard. I feel it is one of the most difficult paths to tread in our schools today. Our children have to fit into schools, not the other way round. I meet only a few children who enjoy mathematics. Therefore, I fail to see the overriding need to teach simultaneous equations or algebraic formula to children who are going to repair computers, or work in a supermarket. Children will learn what they want to learn, from people with whom they con-nect. It could be that the computer repair person or shop worker may return to learning about simultaneous equations as an adult if that area of life becomes important to them. It is rarely important at the age of sixteen except for the fact it is a four-mark question in a GCSE exam.

Dave hates going to school assemblies because he sees them as a complete waste of time. He would rather stay in The Resource and have ten minutes on a computer game where he has to conquer large parts of Europe. Last year Dave agreed to attend one assembly every other week. This year he has stopped going altogether. This had been agreed with his form tutor. The distress caused to Dave by attending assemblies is simply not worth it. There has to be a place for Dave in our education system because he has so much to offer. It is not diffi-cult to be child centred, but it needs an education system that does not take itself too seriously. We can have flexibility and common sense in our schools. These two factors will certainly improve attempts to become more child centred.

Common sense dictates that we have to encourage and guide pupils to get the best possible grades they can at GCSEs. These mea-sures of success are already recognised by society. We must always play to individual strength areas and this is relatively easy within academic subject areas. The creative subjects such as art have always proved valuable subjects for some of our pupils to experience success. However, there is more that makes a person than just certificates. The majority of pupils in The Resource are happy. It is much easier to work alongside happy people than anxious, distressed and unhappy people. A happy person will feel that 'they belong', that they are valued and that their voice is being heard. These are simple truths to aim for in an autism friendly service and a neurotypical friendly service.

The last few weeks in our old school were hard for some pupils. The uncertainties that change brings can be unsettling. We were surrounded by packing cases and the talk was all about our new school and new resource base. Staff encouraged the pupils to write about their memories of the current battered and broken down resource base. One 13-year-old Y8 pupil wrote that he would miss The Resource base because it was the first place where he ever felt really happy. There is a Native American saying that states we do not inherit this earth from our parents rather, we borrow it from our children. Happy children would appear to be a good starting point. Good things will flow from this simple truth.

CHAPTER 4

Supported Employment at Meadowhall

Work experience for our pupils at school has always been very important. Some of our pupils begin a weekly placement from their Y9 (aged between 13 and 14 years old) with full support from a member of staff. The placements are varied to suit individual need although we have never succeeded in finding work experience in a computer games shop (at least one pupil asks for this to be arranged every year). It has always been felt that these placements (which could last three years if successful) are just as important as academic qualifications. Whenever possible, placements are designed to encompass and utilise areas of strength or special interests. As Patricia Howlin suggests (1997), 'it would seem more profitable in the long term for educational programmes to concentrate on those areas in which the person with autism already demonstrates potential competence, rather than focusing on areas of deficit' (p.26).

For Andrew and Shaun, their work experience while at school, proved vital in them both gaining paid employment as adults. The maintenance and growth of self-esteem appears to be directly linked to successful work placements, especially for those pupils who may not be able to 'shine' in formal exams and coursework. Since 1998, our charity has employed an extra member of staff who has supported pupils on work placements and young adults in paid employment such as Shaun and Andrew. Currently, we have pupils on weekly placements in a café, a car showroom, a supermarket and a post office.

Our Y10 pupils (aged 14 to 15 years old) do a two-week block of work experience along with their mainstream peers. It is important vocational work and mainstream educationalists appear to be 'catching up' with this idea.

Temple Grandin (1999) talks about bad jobs for people with high functioning autism or AS such as being cashiers and waiting on tables in a restaurant. She highlights good jobs for visual thinkers such as computer programmers. Good jobs for non-visual thinkers might include accountancy and working in a library. Finally, good jobs for people who have poor verbal skills might include some aspects of retail work, sorting jobs or data entry. Generalisations can be useful providing they are used with care and do not restrict our thoughts and ambitions for individuals. We must always remain open and ready for positive surprises. We have been able to make several generalisations about our young people that could be useful for employers over the last few years and they are listed below:

- liking and need for routine

- liking/need for what others might consider boring or mundane tasks

- ability to learn key tasks that rely on repetition

- if happy – punctual and reliable

- if a coffee break is fifteen minutes – will not take sixteen minutes

- visual/memory skills in key areas

- polite and respectful to colleagues and customers alike

- once routine is established, and if happy, will not leave after six months

- dislike of making mistakes

- will be at work despite having a cold/flu/general sickness/broken leg

- will apply health and safety rules, usually with some rigidity.

If you have ever tried to 'cold sell' something (encyclopaedias, cleaning products or double glazing for example) you will know it is never an easy job. However uncomfortable it may seem, we are at a point in the short history of ASDs where we (parents and professionals) often find ourselves in the position of 'selling' the strengths of someone on the spectrum. Given the very low profile of people with ASDs in our society, and the discrimination towards people with a disability in the employment market, this is a huge and often daunting task. I always try to have some patience with people who are trying to cold sell a 'product' door to door (although like most people, double glazing does get on my nerves a bit).

In many respects, the young people out on work experience and in paid employment are 'guinea-pigs' in terms of autism and society. Perhaps, a better term would be early pioneers. They are in a position to take on the main responsibility for teaching members of the public. This is far from ideal because apart from asking a lot of individuals, it is placing some responsibilities on members of the public who may have not had to confront these issues before. A minority of our young people do not want their employer to know about their ASD. One girl complained to her mother about her work placement at a hairdresser's. The placement itself was great and she had overheard a customer passing on some praise to the manager. The manager agreed with the customer that this girl was an absolutely brilliant worker but then made the mistake of adding, 'and she's autistic you know'. Suffice to say the girl was unhappy about this remark and one of my colleagues went on a visit to have a little chat with the manager. Her reference from this employer was one of the best I have ever read and rightly so.

Our Employment Support Worker always spent a large part of her week travelling between placements. When our charity had to cut this post to part time a few years ago (because of funding), this wasted travelling time became even more evident. It is not rocket science to imagine that having one support worker in a large centre of employment should prove to be more beneficial in a number of respects: they could establish strong links with a greater number of employers, they would have a base, the learning curve for employers and employees involved would be steeper because of a greater presence of workers with an ASD, and transport costs would be lower.

Meadowhall is a large out of town shopping and entertainment centre and it was top of our list. It opened in 1990 three miles north of the city centre and covers 2000 acres. There are eleven major stores, 200 shops, fifteen restaurants, twenty-five catering units, twenty-six speciality stores and an eleven-screen cinema. The company that runs the centre employs over 300 people in full- and part-time jobs such as cleaning, maintenance, hospitality, administrative work and management positions. Your next task is to cold sell the strengths of people with ASD to the owners and management of this centre. We did not even know how to get a foot in the door, but despite the NAS employment service (Prospects) not being interested in the centre, we always felt it was the right thing to try and do. Then the slice of luck came.

A few years ago, we heard of an ex-businessman in Sheffield who had an 'interest' in autism. Norman Adsetts was knighted in 1999 for his services to the community in Sheffield. I wrote to him and he said that he would love to visit some of our pupils on work placements. I took him to Norwich Union and Tesco to see two of our young pupils on their work placements. He seemed to like what we were trying to do and explained that the issues around employment, access and inclusion for people with an ASD were major concerns of his because two of his eight grandchildren are on the spectrum. We bumped into each other a few more times after this at conferences. He is an extremely positive person.

At a similar time we tried to overcome this idea of cold selling the strengths of people with ASDs to people who may not have the time to listen very carefully. It seemed sensible to try to get some of the employers with whom we were currently working, to talk to employers with whom we wanted to work, i.e. Meadowhall. I can speak the 'language of autism' to anyone who will listen, but I cannot speak the 'language of employers'. It seemed that the ability to be bi-lingual would be a distinct advantage. For eleven years we have had gut feelings about when was the right time to tackle something ourselves, and when it was right to look for guidance and help. It was felt that the best way forward was to make a short video about our work with employers. A producer was found through Hallam University and a fee of approximately £10,000 was agreed. For our charity, this was a huge amount of cash, but Trustees felt that a quality film about autism and employment would help to open more doors. It could act as 'an ice-breaker'.

The filming took a lot of extra time and effort. I had never been a 'director' before and it was brilliant fun. The producer, one camera-man and I travelled round to Sainsbury's, Norwich Union and the council's housing department. Hours of film were taken for what eventually turned into a twelve-minute video called 'Building Bridges – Autism At Work'. I learnt a lot. Doing interviews with some of the managers involved and hearing their praise for individual students was re-assuring. Staff arranged a preliminary viewing for parents, pupils and invited friends. About twenty people were expected in a small room above a pub. Treble that number came and we had to have three sittings for the film. The evening turned into another one of those valuable and fun social gatherings that are so important for staff and parents alike. We picked up some valid criticisms and positive suggestions at this meeting about what we could do to improve the film. A friend of ours, Richard Exley, was particularly helpful in stressing that the voices and opinions of the young people themselves needed to have a higher profile in the film. I toddled off with sound recording equipment to do interviews with Andrew and several other young people. My favourite bit on the film is when one of the employers says that people with an ASD will do the most repetitive and mundane of jobs. Later, in an interview with a young man on a placement at Norwich Union he comments that his least favourite job is folding letters to put them into envelopes. When asked why, he replies that this part of the job is boring and tedious. Sir Norman Adsetts kindly agreed to be interviewed as an ex-employer and that is when I discovered that he knew the centre director at Meadowhall. You could have knocked me down with a feather (where on earth did that expression come from?).

Sir Norman spoke to the centre director at Meadowhall to clear the way for me to write to him. The letter was probably one of the best I have ever written because it had to be. I was invited to a meeting with the director. This meeting saw me wear a tie for the second time in eleven years (the first being my interview for the job). The director was brilliant and put me at ease straight away. We had a lovely talk and his head of human resources sat in on part of the meeting. She was given the task of doing an audit to see how many people Meadowhall employed who had a recognised disability. This was one occasion when I cynically hoped for a low percentage. There was no need for me to worry. I left the director with a copy of our first book and we arranged to meet again a month later. At this meeting it would be arranged for myself and two of the Trustees to spend time looking at possible employment areas within Meadowhall.

At the second meeting our video 'Building Bridges' was ready so the meeting began with the director and four of his colleagues watching our film. I was able to relax knowing that the managers on the video, plus Sir Norman Adsetts were all 'speaking the right language'. On the video Andrew's manager at Sainsbury's says that he is polite, punctual and hard working, and that she wished there were 'more like him'. The human resources centre's manager reported back that of the 300 or so employees at Meadowhall, less than 1 per cent had a recognised disability. This does not take into account the 200 or more shops at the centre. Two Trustees and myself then spent a couple of hours with the centre's managers of cleaning, catering and maintenance. These three managers were brilliant. I trailed the maintenance manager and he showed me behind the scenes in a busy shopping centre. The miles of corridors behind the scenes were amazing. We went up on to the roof to look at jobs such as window cleaning. It was a brilliant learning experience. Back in a final meeting with the director later that day, it was agreed that we could certainly help each other. He wanted to see how people with an ASD could work in various areas of Meadowhall and would act as an intermediary between us and the retail outlets. We wanted to put a full-time employment support manager into Meadowhall initially for two years. We needed office space and preferably someone to pay for heating, lighting, publicity and some phone bills. The centre director assured us that this would not be a problem. The costs for an office space, heating, lighting and phone bills comes to over £4000 a year and Meadowhall have kindly helped us out.

It was only when I got hopelessly lost walking back to one of the 12,600 car parking spaces that the gravity of the situation dawned on me. We had worked hard to get the opportunity without taking time to raise the necessary finance for the post itself. Having said that, I guess there are only so many hours in a day, and why let a little thing like money get in the way of a good idea? We always knew that our charity would have to raise the finance for this project.

Trustees discussed the post and agreed that they wanted to pay a salary that would attract a person with the right qualities. The least we could offer was a two-year contract. This was an immense job for anyone to take on and the isolated nature of the post called for a strong person (most likely to be an anorak). I was sent away to find the necessary finance and the bulk of this came from the Lloyds TSB Foundation, The Three Guineas Trust and the Inge Wakehurts Trust. I am sure that the people who are Trustees on these charities and trust funds have little idea about the difference their decisions make. Swathes of disadvantaged groups of people all over the UK depend on monies from charitable sources. All I do is write a thank-you letter and a follow-up report about our projects. It never seems enough somehow. The fact that this charitable finance covers the 'gaps' in statutory funding should continue to be a source of questions and anger in a civilised society. This money for 'worthy causes' papers over the cracks in a society where the rich get richer and the poor and disadvantaged can go to hell (as long as they do it quietly).

There are some things in one's working life that bring an extra sense of pride and fulfilment. The advert for our employment support manager appearing in the local newspapers in Sheffield is one of those moments for me, and the little yellowing piece of newsprint still has pride of place on my study wall. It reads:

A Unique Opportunity in the field of Autistic Spectrum Disorders

Trustees of King Ecgbert Resource would like to appoint an

Employment Support Manager

Initially it is a two-year contract with a salary of between £17,000 and £22,000 depending on experience.

Based at Meadowhall shopping/entertainment centre, this post has been negotiated with the management at Meadowhall and would begin in March 2003.

The person appointed would need to have experience of working alongside people with autism. They would need to have excellent communication skills and be highly motivated. People with autism are under-represented in the employment market. This post is a unique attempt to correct the current unemployment rate of 96 per cent for people with autism in the UK.

Twelve people good, true and brave applied for this post, most of them willing to trade in secure jobs for this unique opportunity. The human resources manager from Meadowhall joined several Trustees to form an interview panel. I am not allowed to be a Trustee (because I work for the LEA) and so had to sit this one out, which, for me, is never easy. The person appointed, Glynis, had worked for four years as a support worker in The Resource. She gave up a permanent post, an additional salary from our charity and her employer's pension contributions to take on an unknown challenge. The equivalent must be diving off the top board blindfolded not knowing whether the water below will be warm or not; in fact not knowing there was any water below at all. I am supposedly the line manager of this post. Glynis is a very strong and self-sufficient person and she accepted this new part of her working life with enthusiasm and a smile. We do not meet enough although usually speak on the phone at least once a week. Glynis has made this part of our work her own, and she has my respect and gratitude. The last time I signed her monthly work sheet, the Trustees owed her about fifty hours in overtime. A true anorak. The lottery bid which was being considered at the time of writing represents her livelihood for the next three years. I try not to think about the lottery bid in this way too often because the reality of failing is very scary. Glynis and 'her boys' have had a ball at Meadowhall over the past two years. There is also no denying the fact that it has been extremely hard work.

Meadowhall is a huge organisation and Glynis had to negotiate her way round various meetings and try to get people on board as quickly as possible. However, above all she had to learn about the structures and people involved. Nothing would happen overnight as we wanted it to. Tact and diplomacy are the main tools of professionals engaged in the business of access and inclusion. And then there was Tom.

Tom had been a pupil at The Resource. Academically, Tom had not been able to shine as society would judge success, although his D grade in Textiles was a miracle in itself. In one of his pieces of research for Textiles, Tom had to look at the materials used for making children's play tents and sleeping bags. A member of staff brought in these two items. On a warm afternoon in The Resource, he got in the tent, curled up in the sleeping bag and dozed off for half an hour. He did three years' work experience for a morning a week at a local supermarket. He went to college and was supported in his NVQ (National Vocational Qualification) in Retail. while at college, he had several successful work placements in the retail sector. The support he received at school and college was good but at the age of 18, it was felt that a job in retail would be a little too stressful for him. Tom reluctantly agreed and was happy to have a look at a cleaning job at Meadowhall. After a couple of interviews with support from Glynis and his wonderful parents, Tom was awarded a six-month probationary period as a cleaner, the same as any other person who starts work at Meadowhall. He was our first young person who gained paid employment at Meadowhall and he is a star. Glynis got to know his supervisor well and had regular meetings with her and Tom about how his work was progressing. The supervisor kept Tom on the same area so that he felt more comfortable. Tom quickly proved that he was reliable, punctual and hard working. His independence grew and Glynis was successful in doing herself out of a job with Tom. Success is when you are not needed as much and ultimately, when you are not needed at all.

However, there were usually issues for Glynis to work on with Tom. A lot of support was given with independent travel and what to do if something 'went wrong'. Tom had an assessment after six months and passed with flying colours. His manager was full of praise. In Tom's six-month appraisal she wrote, 'Tom has fitted in well with the rest of the team. He has put in 100 per cent in all his duties. He has far exceeded what we expected from him when he first started'. His working week went up to 40 hours and this proved a little too much for Tom and so he was permitted to do a 30-hour week. Glynis is there if she is needed by Tom and acts as the first line of communication with his parents. Depending on what shift he is working, Glynis will pop in and have lunch with Tom. Tom's self-esteem continued on its upward curve. When one shift had finished he had a meal at Meadowhall, and then caught the bus to meet a relative so that they could watch his beloved Sheffield Wednesday play a football match. These 'normal' things are momentous days for anoraks and parents alike. The economic factors in this success are what we have to get over to the politicians. For the rest of us, Tom is able to continue learning about the world and other people, and he may be the first person with an ASD that some of his co-workers and managers have ever come across. He is now their teacher and they are privileged to have him as that. With further growth and development, who knows where Tom will be working in a year's time. Perhaps he will get a job in the retail sector or maybe he will take on more responsibility within the cleaning industry.

Tom appeared in our first newsletter to parents. His photograph was followed by an interview with Tom about his experiences at school and in work. He comes on our social evenings and thoroughly enjoys being with his friends. His mother is the secretary for our charity and was a speaker at our last conference. She had never spoken in public before and I can only admire her courage and determination. She talked about the struggle to gain a diagnosis and the terrible treatment her son had from his local primary school. The lack of support from her GP will be well known by other families, but is still shocking for today's parents to hear. There were times when the stresses and strains of looking after Tom and trying to fight for a better future for him must have been crippling. I am lucky to know and learn from such strong people. At the end of her emotional and passionate speech, she talked of 'her working son'. I get choked just remembering that, so we have to return to good hard cold facts before I get criticised as being overemotional. Tom now pays income tax, claims less in benefits and contributes towards his own pension scheme (along with his employer). That saving to the state is not being re-invested in people with ASDs who want to gain paid employment but who cannot face the ignorance and discrimination which still exists. There are many more 'Toms' who need support and guidance if they are to become 'working men'. There are many more mothers who should feel even prouder of their 'working sons'. Ooops: I have slipped into emotional wet blanket state again. Another cold hard fact is that this service, funded through our charity, now has a waiting list.

When The Resource was established at King Ecgbert School in 1994, the telephone rang from Day One from other parents and groups wanting more information. Some wanted access to our educational provision. When our service at Meadowhall was established in 2003, the telephone rang from Day One from other parents and groups wanting more information. Some wanted access to our supported employment service. This is inevitable because there are so few services for adults with ASDs and yet it still amazes me. Glynis had to produce a price list of the services we offer for other people who wanted the teenagers and young adults with whom they worked to gain some experience of employment. This was brilliant for us because we met new people with ASDs who would add to our knowledge base and experience.

One such young man was John. John had been attending an excellent special school until the age of 16. He then attended a catering course at college and as part of this needed a work placement. John has limited speech and is quite rigid in his approach to life. Glynis arranged some work experience in the busy kitchen of an Italian restaurant at Meadowhall. John needed full support in order to survive in this tough working environment. He chopped salad, measured out portions of pasta into storage bags and loaded the dishwasher. He did this for an afternoon a week for over a year and then the placement increased to two sessions a week. John learnt about independent travel and always kept in very close contact with his mother. Glynis built a trusting relationship with the managers of the restaurant and with John. Gradually, over a long period of time, Glynis was able to negotiate some independence with John although she was always on hand if a crisis occurred. I supported John for one afternoon while Glynis took a well-deserved break. I must have lost a few pounds in weight in this hot, oppressive and non-stop environment. John knew what he was doing and for that I was eternally grateful. John is independent at work now and also gets paid for ten hours a week. If you had told me that this would be the outcome for John when he started on the placement eighteen months ago, I would probably have laughed. It would not surprise me given a few more years, if he progressed to being the kitchen manager. He came on one of our social evenings at Christmas and thrashed me at pool. Next time…he's going down!

Not all our experiences have happy endings, but we are all learning as we go along. Bill came through The Resource. Having been predicted F grades in his GCSEs, he managed to get three C grades, two Ds and four Es. Bill progressed to college to study electrical installation. He gave up a bar job for a four-week placement with the maintenance team at Meadowhall. He did well and they gave him a box with some tools in. His new CV looked a little more impressive. He then went for a job as a maintenance engineer in the amusement arcade at Meadowhall. This was his dream job and if he could pass the exams and become accredited, he could work in amusement arcades anywhere in the country. For ten months with Glynis's support, Bill really tried his best. His manager liked him and in areas such as time keeping and punctuality, he was the best. But, the tasks were beyond him on some occasions and an appropriate end was found to the job. Bill's manager and Glynis were in tears, while he was much more matter-of-fact about the whole experience. He quickly picked up paid work in a packing firm over Christmas. Now, he is looking for paid work again. He will be all right because his CV has few blanks on it. Bill has gained valuable experience and is a lovely mature young adult with a great determination to improve himself. When he first came to Meadowhall, Glynis asked him why he had gone for a job in a bar. He replied that it was an ideal place in which to improve his social skills and his eye contact. You can live with that kind of positive approach from an individual.

Through the good and not so good times, we are learning that there is so much to do and such a long way to travel. It is time to include as many people as possible in this process of access and inclusion in the employment market. Bill's manager will be open to working alongside others on the spectrum because of her positive experiences with him and Glynis. Although the job ultimately ended, all the people involved were on the same side. It is not always easy to achieve in the society of today, but no blame was attached, and this kind of situation could happen to anyone.

There was a celebration arranged at Meadowhall to mark the first year of the project. The management at Meadowhall gave us a conference room for free and we invited lots of friends along for the morning. The young people in work were there to greet visitors and later, presented their employer with a framed certificate to mark their contribution to the scheme. The centre director gave a passionate speech about the scheme. Tom and Dave gave a speech about their jobs at Meadowhall. This was their first public speech. Their courage was there for all to see. Some of our funders attended along with Liz Blackman who is the chairperson of the All Party Parliamentary Group on Autism. It was another proud morning for parents and it gave us the opportunity to publicise the scheme.

The lottery money would make the project at Meadowhall secure for a further three years. It would also allow us to place a similar employment support manager into the city centre. There is a great range of employment opportunities within a city centre. More specifically, we feel that there are more opportunities within the office and administrative environment than there are at Meadowhall. The transport links are just as good and the retail sector has benefited from the gradual regeneration of Sheffield city centre during the last few years.

Christmas jobs have been a great bonus for some of our young people at Meadowhall. They might be in a prime position to benefit from paid work at Christmas because of their work placements within the centre. It gives us a chance to meet new employers. Perhaps people are more willing to 'give us a break' if it is only for a few months during the busy festive spending spree. For the young people looking for work, they can provide the necessary 'foot in the door'. They can aid with the transition from being a full-time college student, to the world of paid employment. Paid work looks even better on a CV than a work placement.

DJ went for a Christmas job in one of those toy and gadget type shops. They sold the latest technical all-singing, all-dancing toys. The job was to be a store demonstrator. The idea was that the public would be more likely to buy stuff if they see it in action. We decided with DJ, that only the manager would know about his ASD. DJ is someone who will always include his ASD in his application form. His view is that it is part of him, just like his love of Japanese cartoons. The interviews were in two stages. The first was a group interview with several of the candidates being observed discussing various topics. The second stage took place on the shop floor. DJ and several other candidates were given the task of demonstrating (for 'demonstrating' read, 'playing with') a toy or gadget to prospective customers. The other permanent members of staff were watching and then gave their views to the manager. DJ won hands down. His enjoyment of the toys was natural and honest. His picture appeared in a local newspaper article and his manager commented that, 'not many 18 year olds are as enthusiastic'.

Tom, John, Bill, DJ and others with whom we have worked at Meadowhall have had large amounts of money invested in them through the education system. With experienced support and varying degrees of guidance to suit their individual strengths and needs, the skills they have acquired through education can be transferred to the employment market place with relative ease. My simple logic suggests that if this does not happen, the resources invested during their education could largely go to waste. They could have relied on state benefits throughout their adult life. But, no one would have benefited from this and I expect that their mental health would have been detrimentally affected by long-term unemployment. As Patricia Howlin (1997) points out 'Financial support for early prevention is, in the long term, likely to prove more cost-effective than crisis management in later life. (p.269)'

One of the most difficult arguments to put forward sometimes is that this work has to be carried out by people who know a little about autism and who have supported people with ASDs before. With the best will in the world, and bucketfuls of good intentions and energy, people with no experience in the field usually do more harm than good. That is another one of those arrogant-sounding statements and the only thing I can say in my defence is that among my many faults, arrogance is not one of them. I am notorious for making mistakes and the supported employment scheme at Meadowhall has provided just another arena for clangers to be dropped.

Lee had five years at King Ecgbert School supported by the team I am privileged to know and work with. He found it a challenge to shine through taking exams. Lee was, and remains to this day, one of the deepest thinkers about life and the universe I have ever met. His analytical skills extended from his friendships to the most abstract comedy shows on TV. Lee loves to discuss issues and topics but is also very comfortable in his own company. He became a big supporter of The Resource and all the staff. I never heard him say a bad word about anyone. Lee appeared to be 'comfortable' with us. He got me very frustrated in one French lesson. I was urging him to put up his hand to answer questions because I knew he was aware of the correct responses. He just sat there looking calm and serene. After the lesson, I challenged him about this. He agreed that he knew most of the correct responses, but wanted to give the other children a chance. He was keen to learn about his autism but even more keen to learn about neurotypicals. Lee had a successful work placement on a local farm. At school, we 'lost' him once for about three months. He just stopped talking to us. His body language changed as he became more closed. Staff tried to keep the pressure of communicating away from Lee. We tried not to flap or fuss. The stock cupboard (with the light off) became his favourite place. After a school holiday, he returned as if nothing had happened. We have discussed this episode several times over the years, but no real answers were ever found. Life is full of mysteries and we do not always have to possess 'answers'. Anyway, I digest...back to 'the mistake'.

Lee progressed to college to study an NVQ in Retail. Given the academic and organisational challenges he faced on a daily basis, he was going to find it difficult to progress further than the very basic levels of qualifications. He worked in the college sweet shop and had a work placement at Meadowhall in a large stationery and magazine shop. Here he had to unpack stock and load it onto the right shelves in the correct order. Lee found this too hard sometimes, or so we thought. Despite good levels of support from Glynis, it was felt that the retail sector was just too demanding for Lee to cope with. Lee came to see me at school and his overriding desire was to find some paid employment. He was not keen on returning to college. Neither Lee nor his parents were very open to looking at alternative careers. Without wanting to appear ungrateful in any way, Lee's parents felt that retail was his best option and they would not consider alternatives such as cleaning. Lee was open to any suggestions we made, but was trying to consider the feelings of his parents at the same time. By this time we had seen the great steps forward that Tom had made with the cleaning department at Meadowhall and Lee decided to think about a cleaning post. We knew there were people within the cleaning department who would be patient and positive with Lee.

Lee and I met at Meadowhall to attend an interview for a trial period as a cleaner. Once again, one of my ex-pupils was dressed more smartly than me. No offence to Lee, but I felt that he did not do his best at the interview. He was a little uncommunicative and I was a little uncomfortable. Despite this he was rewarded with a job and they even changed their shift pattern around so that Lee could work the hours he wanted. Result – or so I thought.

Soon after this, Lee's father saw that Marks and Spencer (a large department store) at Meadowhall was advertising their Christmas vacancies. The posts all included working on the checkout tills. He arranged an interview for his son. His parents told us that this was happening and I suppose we felt that Lee stood little chance of getting one of these posts. Lee attended the interview with his father and was charming, articulate and engaging (according to one person on the interview panel). He was given a job and his parents expected (quite rightly) that Glynis would offer her support. Lee was to do a four-hour shift and work five days a week. Christmas at Meadowhall is not the place you would want to be if you crave peace and solitude. After one week in the job our opinion of Lee's chances of success had not altered.

Working on the cash tills at Marks and Spencer during the Christmas period was deemed by the management to be one of the most stressful jobs in the store, and no employee was to do more than an hour at a time. Lee received some training and Glynis was able to repeat any areas that he found difficult. It was decided that he would be better on the till that was for five items or less, although this could be for cash, cash cards and vouchers. After a couple of weeks of learning on the job, and from Glynis, Lee started to do well. His mistakes began to get fewer. His determination to succeed was remarkable and something that Lee had kept well hidden for many years. Some memories will always remain more vivid than others. Glynis phoned me at work one morning. She told me that she was watching Lee serve customers. He was doing the job in front of her eyes. This was a young man who passed his GCSE Maths at the lowest possible grade and did not take any formal exams in English. Lee did not want to leave his till after an hour and there were occasions when he remained at his post for up to three hours. This was a more satisfying position for Lee than stacking shelves. Lee found stacking shelves hard but could never articulate this to us for several reasons. First, he rightly considered that shelf stacking was part of the job and therefore it had to be done (however badly). Second, one of Lee's major strengths is his charm. He does not like to upset people. What he says to someone may not exactly match how he is feeling. Third, Lee's spatial awareness meant that he could not always see the gaps on shelves or recognise different sizes of the same product. Finally, Lee loved the staff from The Resource. He did not want to let us down. Lee wanted to be 'part of the show' and if this meant stacking shelves, or being a cleaner, then so be it. For Lee, doing something would be better than being stuck at home doing very little.

His Christmas job ended and Lee is now unemployed. His supervisor thought that Lee was a permanent member staff at the store until the week he was leaving and he had to fill in the exit forms. Lee is next on the waiting list should a similar job arise in the department store. I have every confidence that Marks and Spencer will employ Lee in the very near future. In the longer term, I now believe that Lee will learn how to cope with the other complex issues of operating a cash register. Lee continues to be philosophical about the meaning of life and the universe. He always supports any social or fund-raising activities we organise. It is almost as if he is there to guide and watch over me. Each time I see him I cannot help but feel that he is very much my teacher and that I should remember to be open, honest and ready to learn from him. That is all he needs.

Mistakes such as this one are always valuable learning experiences (that is what I believe and I am sticking to it). I stopped beating myself with a big stick a long time ago. As Luke Jackson says, it's OK to be different; the same is true of making mistakes. People with ASDs make mistakes because they have to live and function in a neurotypical world. I make mistakes in my work with people with ASDs because I am not autistic. I get better at mind reading but it is never an exact science. I know a man with an ASD who is in his early thirties. He has had five different disability employment advisors in the last two years and still no paid work. I would make fewer mistakes than these five advisors, full of good intentions as I am sure they are.

Meadowhall has been a fantastic experience for all involved. We could not have predicted where the successes would come but we knew they would. This knowledge comes from having faith and understanding about the strengths of the young people we work alongside. I wish I could spend more time at Meadowhall but I would only stand around and watch friends work with a big smile on my face. Glynis wants advice on how to 'switch off' from the job. I am not sure that I am the right person to ask about that. Parents do not have the luxury of switching off in the first place. The project is a success largely because of Glynis and the hard work and sheer determination which she has shown. She continues to stand up and speak for the young people with the whole force of her personality. We do not agree on everything, but life would be dull if we did. She is the expert in terms of supporting people with ASDs at Meadowhall and I am lucky to be able to learn from her. The people at Meadowhall from the cleaners to the management have been accommodating and kind. They have developed their understanding about ASDs by learning from the young people themselves. We have watched from nearby, as they have been pleasantly surprised. We have been on hand when they have needed to ask additional questions. They are now in a position to contribute their own ideas and suggestions. They have become active partners.

One young man at Meadowhall has a placement at Boots. He was asked by his supervisor to clear a pallet of drinks onto the shelves. This was a daunting task as the pallets were stacked quite high and each pack of bottles was heavy. He got half way through the job and sighed. Glynis (who was supporting him at the time) asked him if he was tired. 'Oh no,' he replied, 'this job just keeps getting better and better.' Some of the younger pupils in The Resource ask about Meadowhall and what they might do when they are older. There is no doubt that for some pupils, Meadowhall is where they plan to work. Given the current situation, I cannot make any positive assurances for these pupils. All I can do is send them off to their next lessons, or their work experience placements and hope that it will not be all in vain.

CHAPTER 5

Hot Sand, Itchy Clothes, Screaming People, Total Darkness

There are times when even the best child-centred approaches, and the most flexible support within a secondary school can be stretched and challenged to the limit. These are the times when it is more important to listen rather than talk. As a neurotypical person, I will hold my hands up and say that I struggle to comprehend the sheer terror and fear that sensory factors can play in the life of someone with an ASD. I know a little more now than before I met Hamish. Hamish and his loving parents gave my learning curve a real kick up the rear. This chapter is my poor attempt to prevent professionals from merely paying lip service to sensory factors within ASDs. It is written with approval from Hamish. He wants people to know about the struggle and torment that is his life. He will be a success in his chosen field one day and I want to be there when he earns his first million pounds, or gets the Nobel Peace Prize (or preferably both).

As a 3-year-old, Hamish was very interested in refuse collection. He liked to follow the bin lorry round his locality. He would be up at 6 a.m. to play with toy figures that represented bin men, their lorry and the dustbins. His parents viewed this, quite rightly, as perfectly normal behaviour for a 3-year-old. On more than one occasion the living room was buried under mounds of tiny polystyrene balls (like the ones used in packaging), which represented the rubbish in

Hamish's routine. Only one incident really stands out in these early years. While being pushed in his buggy, Hamish and his mother passed a road-sweeping lorry. He screamed at the noise this lorry produced. It is only with the benefit of hindsight that his mother now thinks this screaming was beyond what one might have considered 'normal'.

Hamish did not have a diagnosis when he was suicidal during his final year at primary school (aged 11). When the diagnosis came (which matched closely with Asperger's Syndrome), it was not until the end of his first year at secondary school. Hamish is academically bright. In his Y6 SATs, he gained two level 5s in Maths and Science and a level 4 in English. He survived for two weeks in his mainstream secondary school before it all began to get too much for him. It was at this point that I met Hamish's mother who travelled several hundred miles to attend an open evening at King Ecgbert. There was no Statement of Special Educational Needs for Hamish and so he received no additional support. With hindsight, it is a miracle that he survived during this period. I am sure he still carries the scars.

Hamish and his family moved to Sheffield in 2001 because the services for people with ASDs were underdeveloped where they lived. There was still no Statement although it was being written. Hamish went to a good special school in Sheffield while some assessments were carried out. He could not have coped in a mainstream secondary school at this point. His attendance at the special school was patchy to say the least. The journey to and from school in a minibus seemed to make him tired and irritable. He came to visit The Resource with a member of staff from the special school. Hamish appeared calm, communicative, in control of himself, articulate and intelligent. He did yawn a bit but I put this down to stress (because his mother had warned me about this trait) and the fact that I do babble on sometimes.

It was decided, given that Hamish now had a Statement, that he should attend King Ecgbert and that we would offer support. He slotted into a high set in Maths and Science and a more able group in English. He did not want to attend lessons in French or Music, and PE would be left flexible depending on what activity was taking place. Hamish also had tremendous strengths within IT. He had about five

to six hours a week in The Resource. He did not do the school sponsored walk due to having problems with walking. Hamish brought
his own lunch from home, the content of which was always identical.
The minibus journey appeared to be fine and the escort and driver
(Brenda and Tony) were brilliant. Hamish's attendance was high during his first year (his Y9, when he was aged 13). Everything seemed
fine at school and we were just beginning the inevitable process of
questioning what all the fuss was about. He made friends, and at
lunchtime in The Resource there was a gaggle of about ten teenagers
with Hamish being very much 'part of the scene'. In his Y9 SATs,
Hamish got two level 6s, in Maths and Science and a level 5 in English. We were getting the structure right for Hamish. We began to pat
ourselves on the back. If we could achieve this in such a short space of
time, then anybody could do it. It was a long way from being stress
free, but rocket science it most certainly was not. Then the communication from home about Hamish began to take on certain patterns.
His parents began to get used to the fact that they could be honest
with us about home life with Hamish (and his three other siblings).

Home life was a nightmare for Hamish and all the family. It is difficult to portray this and I can only think that other parents will read
this and nod in knowing acknowledgement. Professionals have got
to recognise the complete 'non lives' that people like Hamish can
cause at home for every member of their family. The bond of love
between Hamish's mum and dad is stronger than anything I know. I
remember the TV programme about Luke Jackson and his family
being shown on the BBC in 2003. I drove to school the next morning eagerly looking forward to asking Hamish what he thought
about the programme. Hamish looked particularly downcast and
when I asked about the programme, his reaction was that life in families where there was a person with an ASD could not possibly be that
good. The programme portrayed a happy family sitting round the
table having meals together. His opinion was that the BBC had only
shown 'the good bits'.

The only respite Hamish's parents had at home was when he was
ensconced on the computer. The internet was Hamish's world and
one where he could excel. He played strategy games in addition to a
mean battle of chess. The great days at school were only good on the

surface. Hamish was surviving at school and letting rip at home. He could not be left alone with his brothers and sister. They were noisy and unpredictable, and Hamish was ready to physically hurt them (and often did). While his mum got the dinner ready, his dad would have to 'stand on guard' and vice versa. The family walked around on eggshells and this was still too loud for Hamish.

Hamish was talking about things that stressed him from years before. Mealtimes were a non-starter. He could not eat with the rest of the family because of the noise of knives and forks banging together. The sound of his family actually chewing food was too loud. He would only eat bland foods. Strong smells such as bacon would agitate him to distraction. At one point the noise of his own eating would cause distress. Certain clothing such as shell suits were too noisy for Hamish. All his own clothes had to be soft material like brushed cotton. Light of any kind (natural or artificial) appeared to hurt Hamish. He was having frequent and severe headaches.

At home, Hamish's parents quickly realised there could be no 'dead time'. Every waking minute needed to be accounted for so that Hamish knew what was going to happen. The whole workings of the family home had to operate with Hamish's needs being uppermost. His siblings could not have their friends around unless they were as quiet as mice. His own birthday was unbearable because it created anxiety due to change and transition. It was not to be mentioned. The birthdays of his siblings were equally difficult. It was as if Hamish had a huge force field around himself. He had little insight into what was happening and his parents were continually playing 'mind games' to try and establish any kind of patterns to make all of their lives a little more manageable.

Sleep was elusive for Hamish and therefore his parents. He would have great difficulty falling asleep and tended to rove around the house disturbing everyone else. He could not communicate what was happening, but worse, he could not 'shut down' at night. Herbal medicines were tried and then melatonin, which did have positive effects. In the daytime, Hamish was continually tired and his pallor was paler than a ghost's. In addition to sensory challenges, Hamish is quite open with his opinions and is frequently blind to the effect they might have on other people. A friend of the family bought Hamish's mum some beautiful flowers. Hamish expressed the view that flowers were a waste of money and that the cash would have been far more useful to the family.

Parents of children who have different sensory experiences to neurotypical children can read on now. Professionals within the field of autism need to go back and re-read the last five paragraphs. This time you actually have to imagine how debilitating life was in this household. Imagine being physically disturbed by light, smells, touch and noises like the rustling of a sweet paper. Hamish's mother tells of waiting for a bus in Sheffield town centre. Hamish became distressed because he could hear people eating crisps the other side of a six-foot high wall. Hamish was in a car with his dad and became distressed because a shopkeeper was sweeping his shop front just as they passed. Bend down low, get nearer and feel the strain in this household. The tears and frustrations far outweighed any hollow sounds of laughter. Remember the extreme pain next time you are working with a child that covers their ears, or recoils when you brush past them. The rules are different. Even if we listen and remain open to being taught, we can only gain a partial understanding of what Hamish (and other children like him) go through on a minute-by-minute basis.

At this point, Hamish was not in any kind of position to be able to 'teach' us about what he was going through. Subconsciously, I am sure he did not think that anyone would take him seriously, let alone try to help. The mistakes were frequent and the results were seen by Hamish disappearing to his room, under his duvet, for hours, then days and finally, weeks at a time. Sometimes, however experienced a person is, there is a tendency to look for 'fixed' answers. However understanding and empathic a person is, once this 'fixed mentality' gets a grip, it is not good. More serious mistakes will be inevitable. This downward and outward spiral of errors is destructive, blinkered and yet very human. Working within an education system that is restrictive and inflexible can exacerbate this process. Creative think-ing is not easy within the tight structure of a secondary school. The biggest mistake I made was in getting further and further into this autism/non autism 'battle' which resulted in me drawing a line in the sand and in thinking that I could not retreat from my position anymore.

I felt that every conceivable concession had been made at school for Hamish. Nothing was making a great deal of difference to his home life and I was not sure where else we could take pressure away. Some other pupils within The Resource already thought that Hamish was onto a 'cushy number', in the way he was treated differently. During Y10 (when they are aged 14 to 15), the pupils have to give a number of 'speeches' that count towards their overall GCSE grade for English. These speeches could be on a favourite film, or things they would rid the world of, or future ambitions and dreams. Hamish had full support in these English lessons while the speeches were planned and further work was done in The Resource. The experience of standing in front of his peers was going to be stressful so it was agreed Hamish could deliver his speech from his usual chair. The build-up to the first speech was slow and stressful. Hamish felt that it was too much to ask. The stresses built at home. Staff arranged it so that Hamish would give his speech to just the teacher and support worker. Then it became just the support worker. For the second speech, I thought that progress could be made and insisted that Hamish's English teacher be in on the act. Big mistake because by this time I had turned a stressful situation for Hamish into a personal struggle. I used all my powers of persuasion to talk the issues through with Hamish. The only effect was for Hamish to become increasingly distraught and tearful. The second speech was never given and Hamish was off school for several weeks.

In effect this brought his good start to Y10 crashing down. Hamish spent less time in mainstream lessons and more time either in The Resource base, or at home. The friends he had made began to fade away. Hamish did remain friends with a couple of lads with Asperger's Syndrome in The Resource. However, the stresses were increasingly evident. One pupil in The Resource had a cough that seemed to last for a period of months. It was a quiet cough to most people. Hamish would complain bitterly that this pupil was coughing on purpose just to annoy him. On the minibus, he would complain about the noise of the younger children, or 'the midgets' as he called them. However, he could shut himself off by reading. Hamish is an avid reader. He likes fantasy books, history, politics and his beloved Terry Pratchett. One social activity he liked was to play chess.

A trip into town was arranged with a support worker because we needed to buy some new games for the computers. Hamish was put in charge of purchases, a role he took to with great seriousness. He had to canvass the opinions of other pupils to see what kind of computer games they would like. His motivation for this trip was high and served to remind staff that progress could be made as long as we push 'the right buttons'. The pace was slow by our standards, and was dictated by Hamish, but there were early signs that we were learning and being more receptive to his world of fears and pains. Despite the fact that Hamish finds mealtimes difficult, he adores Pizza Hut. He would tolerate this dining extravaganza with his mother or father because his motivation (the quality pizza) was high. However, he still complained about the music played in such eating establishments and to their credit, the staff made an effort to help by turning it off.

Towards the end of his Y10, Hamish posed a challenge that is difficult for anyone outside of autism to understand. These challenges had always been present, it is just that parents and staff at school were now much more acutely aware of them. When Hamish was at his most stressed, he would talk to you. Staff would have hours of conversation with Hamish. These talks would include other pupils and anyone else who expressed an opinion. Often, Hamish would dominate these conversations so that he could dictate their direction and content. People with 'right-wing' views would receive his best and most articulate verbal assassinations. These interesting and lively discussions served to mask, or deflect some underlying stress or agitation. Hamish may not even have recognised the causes of the agitation he was feeling at the time. His mother began to recognise this pattern of events at home before we did. As usual, it was a mother who began to piece together important pieces of Hamish's jigsaw.

Hamish's mother began to 'empower' him by asking very specific leading statements at these times of stress. First, his feelings were legitimised by her saying to Hamish, 'you're stressed'. Phrased as a question, 'you're feeling stressed aren't you?' would not work for several reasons. If it was phrased as a question it would put Hamish under pressure. To include the word 'feeling' (e.g. 'you're feeling stressed aren't you?') would just serve to confuse Hamish because 'feelings' are an abstract concept. You are either stressed or not stressed. Short snappy sentences that reflected his feelings like, 'you're upset', began to help unlock some of the emotions that Hamish was going through, or reflecting on. The questions could never be closed but had to be leading ones. These prompts always had to be started by his mother. She could then make attempts to interpret what Hamish said and most importantly, believe him. The best time to do this appeared to be when his mum was driving because this, through necessity, avoided direct eye contact with her son. Hamish was always in charge once these conversations started and he decided when to terminate them. Each time these nuggets of revelation occurred, their relationship and bond of trust grew ever deeper. As usual, there were no short cuts, and nothing appeared conventional. But gradually, during the course of that year, Hamish began to teach us all about the conflicts, pain and incessant nature of the way in which he experienced the world around him. At the same time, his social and academic progress at school came to an abrupt standstill.

Early in his Y11, it became apparent that there was nothing to be gained by Hamish going to any of his lessons at school. His attendance levels were abysmal anyway. The academic content of Maths, English, Science and IT was not the problem. He could have passed GCSEs in those subjects with C grades or above. The sensory factors involved in overloading Hamish's senses of sight and hearing were the stumbling blocks to accessing a mainstream curriculum in the classroom. Hamish did not want to come to school. His parents came to talk to us to make some kind of deal that would at least enable them to have some respite from the deteriorating situation at home. It was decided that Hamish would come to school for three mornings each week on the minibus, and that one of his parents would pick him up before lunchtime. Hamish, who is still bound by rules, saw this as being 'the law', even though he did not want to attend school.

Break times became a sensory challenge because of The Resource being a safe haven for other pupils during this period of transition. Hamish did not like the noise or movement of the other pupils. A separate room was provided for these times with the natural light blocked out by paper stuck on the windows. He did make limited use of this room, although he did not like to be seen going into it because of what others might think. Hamish would read in his room and listen to music with headphones on. The headaches were still severe, but the wearing of skiing glasses reduced the pain of natural and artificial light.

In any area where his motivation was high, Hamish would still attempt to overcome all of his fears and sensory bombardments. He wanted to do a programming course in IT but there was not a suitable one at school. He enrolled at college to do a basic programming course. Hamish is not a good traveller and this evening course meant a long car journey with his father, who then had to stay as well. The lecturer had quite a loud voice that disturbed Hamish. However, once this lecturer saw the skill level and potential Hamish possessed, he wisely allowed him to work at his own speed. It was all right for a while, and at least got Hamish out of the house a bit more often.

The situation in the family home was becoming intolerable for Hamish and his siblings, not to mention Mum and Dad. Early in Hamish's final year at school, they made a decision to become 'voluntary' single parents. Hamish's father worked at a conference centre where he was part of a team that managed the grounds. A flat in the grounds became available and Hamish and his father moved into it with great speed. This entailed his father being on call for an extra three evenings a week. His mother remained at home with the siblings. That all sounds like a nice solution, but the upheaval to this family was immense. A normal, loving marriage was temporarily put on ice. The time span was that this flat was available for about eight months. There was neither Plan B nor any idea of what would happen after this time.

The organisational factors were complex, but managed with the smoothness and efficiency of a well-oiled machine. Adaptations to the flat were quickly made, like covering the natural light coming in through a window in the roof. During times when Hamish could simply not function because of the stresses of sensory overload, he would just lie down on his bed under his duvet cover. These de-stressing periods could last for days at a time.

Every Monday morning at this conference centre, there was a fire drill. Hamish and fire drills do not mix. The uncertainty of whether it is a practice or a real fire, the siren's noise and the movement of people are all too much for Hamish to cope with. At school, we had to be pre-warned of any fire drill. Then we had to either get Hamish out of school, or ring his parents to come and pick him up. Children will be children, and when the fire alarm at school was set off intentionally, Hamish would suffer for weeks afterwards. Pre-warning certain children about a known fire practice at school is still something we do for one or two pupils. They are fine if they know it is going to happen, and will certainly not tell other children about the impending disruption to lessons. The smoke sensors in our new school are so sensitive that we have had four accidental fire drills in seven weeks. One was caused in The Resource kitchen by overheated margarine in a cooking lesson. Some of our pupils were becoming anxious when staff were using the toaster or grill at lunchtime to prepare their snack. We have now covered the smoke sensor and certain pupils remind staff to waft a towel over the toaster when it is being used. Professionals in the health and safety industry can now take their fingers out of their ears. Sometimes rules in this non-autistic world are made to be broken.

At the conference centre where Hamish and his father were living, his mother would arrive at an appointed time before the fire drill to remove him to a safe distance. Apart from this disturbance, life at the flat in the grounds of a conference centre suited Hamish. It was quiet and peaceful. Hamish began to watch TV with the sound on very quietly. Using the toilet at school or in the flat remained an issue. Boys' toilets in any secondary school, however academically successful, are still quite literally, smelly places. Nobody could blame Hamish for not wanting to use them at school. He was provided with a key to a staff toilet. I have my doubts as to whether or not he ever used it because he was too self-conscious to be seen unlocking the door. On returning home or to the flat, if Hamish needed to use the toilet, other members of the family would be encouraged to wait outside.

Hamish did not sit any GCSEs although academically, they would have been a stroll in the park for him. Far more important was the issue of where Hamish would go to after he left King Ecgbert School. We had been alerting the LEA (Local Education Authority), Social Services and the Careers Service since Hamish's Y10 Annual Review. Hamish's parents had been exploring services for people with Asperger's Syndrome and their search was countrywide. Hamish could not attend a college in Sheffield even with full support. Support was never one of the issues, it was all about the environment and having people around him who were open enough to learn from him. Hamish needed to see some of the facilities on offer himself. Some places were very clear that they could not cope with such sensory challenges. Some places said they could manage, and would like to meet Hamish. These places, some of which were purposely advertised as specialising in services for people with AS, were usually at the far ends of the country.

Travelling has never been easy for Hamish, because it is too unpredictable and too noisy. No mode of transport is easy. These trips entailed either a long car journey during which he often becomes sick because of the constant stopping and starting, or travelling by train. In a car, Hamish is also on constant alert for possible siren sounds. Listening to Classic FM or political programmes makes it easier as long as he can sit in the front with only him and the driver in the car, and suck Polo mints. Trains are worse, even though tickets and seats can be booked in advance. The stress of getting in the right coach, and into the correct seats is still an immense achievement for Hamish, and the discussions about any such trip would not have diminished the build up in pressure he must have felt. Train stations are noisy, with people talking and lots of mobile phones ringing. There is the additional worry that someone might be sitting in your pre-booked seat. Once on the train, in the right seat, Hamish can bury himself in a good book, or listen to his walkman CD player. Little signs of stress still remain like twiddling his hair or repetitive leg movements. In times of greater stress, Hamish will peel skin from his fingers or toes.

One such trip led to a residential college for students with AS in the South of England. The train journey was long, and on arrival in a taxi, Hamish took a lot of encouragement to get out and view the place. He was already exhausted from the sensory stimulation of the long journey. Potential students were also arriving and one of the first activities laid on was a kind of circle time where staff could meet the young people and get to know them a little better. You can probably guess by now that Hamish would simply not entertain this notion, and in fact believed that the assumption that he would cope with this situation was laughable. A second distressing factor in this place was the beautiful wooden floorboards that creaked with every footstep. Every factor appeared highly arousing to Hamish. It was the opposite of what he needed but added to our ever-steeper learning curve. It took several days of 'duvet time' back in the flat for Hamish to recover from this.

Hamish was 16 and so did not fall under the auspices of adult Social Services. Social Services have a Transition Team to manage the transfer from child to adult services. All kinds of wonderful assessments could be carried out to see what a particular person will need. However, because of the sheer pressure of numbers, the main assessment tool for this team appears to be a brief look at the Statement of Special Educational Needs. This same team within Social Services has just written to three sets of parents of Y9 pupils (who were aged 13 to 14) at The Resource to inform them that their sons are no longer deemed 'disabled' under some Act of Parliament or other. Their evidence for doing this, you guessed it, the Statement. If you are deemed 'not disabled' as a 14-year-old, you will not require assessments by Social Services after leaving school. I would really like to meet the policy makers who make such decisions and pass them down to their middle managers to carry out. I realise that they have different priorities to me, and I can only hope that they spend a little less time in meetings and more time actually working back in the 'front line'. I would like to introduce them to Hamish, some of my other friends, and their parents.

Hamish's case was complicated further by the continuing involvement of the Area Health Department and by the fact the Learning Skills Council (the state's post-16 educational funder) would also have to be included in any discussion about the future. Hamish was also entitled to some money from the LEA because of his Statement, which gives a funding entitlement up to the age of 19. Each representative from these areas of local government knew there would be a funding implication for any decision regarding Hamish's future after he left school. They also knew that this would not be a 'regular' September start as Hamish and his father would have to be out of their flat by the previous June.

A wonderful provision was located by the parents for Hamish in Scotland. Moorpark was a new community of purpose-built homes for people diagnosed as having ASDs and who require care and support in a progressive learning environment. It sounded too good to be true. Two members of staff from Moorpark came down to Sheffield to listen to our ramblings about what Hamish would need. To their credit, that is exactly what they did do – listen. Hamish did not want to meet them at this point and that seemed to be fine with them. There was no 'hard sell', just a desire to gain as much as possible from the countless mistakes we had made. There was no need for these mistakes to be repeated.

The manager of the Transitions Team in Sheffield Social Services gave me a call about Hamish and the looming crisis. I know this manager and she is passionate about her work and incredibly thorough. She rightly felt that Sheffield should be able to establish its own service for Hamish and that this would be a considerably cheaper alternative than Moorpark. Everything she said made perfect sense. Two factors made her point of view worthless. First, she had not met Hamish and nor was this possible/desirable. Second, there was nowhere suitable for Hamish within the boundaries of Sheffield. I failed miserably in my attempt to explain to her the pain and fear that is Hamish's daily struggle with life. However, what she did agree to do was visit to talk with Hamish's mother. To her credit, she spent an afternoon with Hamish's mum. She succeeded where I had failed. Or maybe we were a strong double act. The manager phoned the next day to say that we were right. Nowhere in Sheffield was suitable for Hamish and she would do her best to sort out the necessary funding. While there are managers who are willing to listen, learn and then act, vulnerable people like Hamish, and their families stand a chance of gaining the services they need. I remain indebted to this manager and the wonderful social worker that was appointed to Hamish's case. They fought like demons to make everything happen.

Hamish went to visit Moorpark and gave his (very small) nod of approval. He would be one of the first people to be resident at

Moorpark. Their openness and willingness to learn was more attractive than the superb accommodation and learning environment. Unlike some other residential provisions, they actually wanted Hamish to go and live in their community. I cannot begin to imagine what that must have felt like for Hamish's parents. The often-seen shakes of the head, and sharp intakes of breath were replaced by re-assurances that they could continue to encourage Hamish to reach his potential. Moorpark promises an autism friendly service with resources and opportunities to enable individuals to maximise their strengths within a safe and motivating environment. The staff are skilled and experienced within the field of autism. Individuals are encouraged to develop their potential, and take responsibility for their own lifestyles. If Hamish wanted to access a programme of learning at 2 a.m., then it would not be a problem.

His house, in which only he lives, is wonderful. It is small, clean, new and safe. It has broadband internet access. The heating system is under the floorboards, which makes it quieter.

Hamish has now been at Moorpark for one year. In the first five weeks, Hamish's mother lived nearby to help him to settle in. She then had one week at home before returning to Moorpark for one further full week. Then his father stayed for one week. For the next eight months, the visits to see Hamish were every other weekend. Now, the visits are one weekend a month.

There is always progress to be made in anyone's life. Hamish is no different. He cooks for himself, although his diet remains quite restricted. Bathing remains a slight problem because of his fears of the noise of running water, and that the bath might overflow. He worries about things like the fridge door not being properly closed. Although the soundproofing in his house is superb, Hamish is still disturbed by noises elsewhere. He can hear fridge doors closing in the house next door to his. Hamish always had the potential to be a nocturnal being. He tends to rise late in the afternoon and then be up for most of the night working on his various projects. This is not a problem for the staff at Moorpark because Hamish is responsible for his own lifestyle and choices. Having money remains a difficult area for Hamish because money represents choice. It can often be spent quickly just to get the decision over with. This can lead to some rash purchases. In other respects, Hamish's social development continues at his pace. He remains fiercely anti-American and anti-royal. He is a big Michael Moore fan and now prefers classical music. He hates any kind of injustice.

One evening a week, Hamish's grandparents visit as they live relatively nearby. They play cards together in Hamish's house. He is an expert rummy player. The relationship between Hamish and his grandparents is stronger than ever before. They enjoy each others' company. I would imagine that not many teenagers have such a close bond with their grandparents. Hamish is rightly proud of his new home and looks forward to the visits of his grandparents.

Hamish's Social Worker has to do an assessment of the first year at Moorpark. Her department has to be satisfied that they are getting best value for the money it costs. Some professionals are concerned that the authorities are paying a lot of money for this place. Moorpark is not cheap. Some argue that because Hamish is not accessing any direct educational input, mainly staying alone in his house, not really wanting to access the skilled and experienced counselling on offer, and generally being considered 'low maintenance' then this high financial cost cannot be justified. For once, I agree with them. Moorpark, however benevolent, has to pay its staff and the running costs of the place. I can only imagine that at some point (if not already) it has to make a profit. Inevitably, this Social Worker then has to look at alternatives. To set up a similar provision in terms of quality would require substantial investment from Social Services in Sheffield. 'Substantial investment in services', and 'Social Services' are not words one often sees combined within the same sentence. The private sector will make these kinds of investment in services, and then reap the benefits. However much I personally dislike this situation, little appears to be done to change it. Moorpark has a high financial cost to Sheffield Social Services in terms of Hamish's placement, but nothing is to be gained by professionals moaning about it. The choice is clear: develop a range of supported living schemes in your own locality or be quiet and pay the ever-spiralling bill.

Hamish has contacts all over the world. When the motivation is high, Hamish will create, discuss, invent and develop. His ideas are immense. When he is working towards a goal that motivates him, he is conscientious, committed and reliable. This level of motivation appears to override the sensory challenges he faces. He still needs time to recover if he has done something that has bombarded his senses, but this will not stop him from inventing something wonderful. Large companies and businesses will be queuing up for his ideas, and I know that the bidding war will be fierce.

Rhonda Prouse, Hamish's Team Leader at Moorpark has written the following:

> When Hamish first arrived at Moorpark he could not communicate with staff as this would have caused extreme anxiety, depression and withdrawal. All communication with Hamish was directed through his parents. During times of anxiety, Hamish would not eat at all. Shopping would need to be put away while Hamish was in his room as he found the noise of the bags unbearable. This was the same for washing dishes and clothes. Hamish was unable to bring himself to explore his new environment either because it was too bright outside, or because of the fear of meeting people and fear of the unknown. He found it difficult having (in his mind) noisy neighbours.

> His quality of life has improved. With understanding of how Hamish's AS affects him, staff were able to create a person-centred care plan that would best meet his needs. This plan was introduced gradually and at a pace that was dictated by Hamish. It was only when Hamish had built some trust in staff that we began to see some signs of progress. Hamish spends large parts of the day on his computer talking with friends. He is eating a greater variety of foods, and sometimes permits staff to prepare meals for him. He regularly goes to the cinema, although it is always the same one, which has a lower level of sensory stimulation.

> Hamish can now tolerate the noise of his washing machine while he is in the same room. He feels safe in his environment and knows what to expect. The noises from his neighbours are now less disturbing because he is more used to them. He regularly goes to Pizza Hut and recently sat through a meal even though there was a child crying at a nearby table. He feels safe with

members of staff and also knows he can return home whenever he wants to. Hamish lets staff run a bath for him three times a week. He has recently taken up golf but only with a particular member of staff with whom he feels most comfortable. He is a little more accepting of new staff in his care team.

Hamish has achieved so much in a year, and there is so much more he wants to do. However, we can never be complacent or underestimate the severity of his AS. We still often feel that Hamish makes two steps forward and we knock him three steps back because staff have pushed too hard, or introduced something too quickly.

The last words in this journey so far, really do belong to his parents. Their learning curve has been of Everest proportions. They have moved from little understanding of, or relationship with their son, to a position of belief, trust and communication. I have been privileged to be a passenger on this journey of self-discovery.

The one thing that Hamish would like to have written in capital letters all over the world is that what he is experiencing is not MILD. He wants you, the reader, to know that just because he is articulate and knowledgeable about certain things, it doesn't mean that he isn't in a constant state of anxiety and sometimes terror. He has come to believe that those people on the autistic spectrum who are non verbal and express themselves by maybe biting, hitting and screaming have an advantage over him. Why? Well, because it is obvious when they are distressed or over aroused. When things are obvious, people take you absolutely seriously. Hamish, however, can feel unnoticed when he is distressed. When Hamish complains that the noise someone's coat makes is upsetting him, it is hard to read the level of his distress from the tone of his voice or his demeanour. We might just acknowledge him and carry on with what we are doing when in fact he either needs us to rip the noisy coat off its owner and burn it, or to have an emergency team rush in with a stretcher and swiftly carry Hamish away to a quiet sanctuary!

After many years, we have come to understand that when Hamish is over-aroused he can seem to become more engaged with life, more interested, more chatty, more cheerful and charming. We have often been seduced into believing that Hamish is feeling comfortable and at ease with life. How wrong we were. When he appears at his most conventional he is actually at his most vulnerable and needs to be rescued immediately.

I remember a long train journey that we had together. I was very aware that Hamish would be on sensory overload with all the noises, smells and bright lights in the station and on the train. I had taken on my Red Alert pose but found myself gradually relaxing and enjoying Hamish's non-stop lively company. It took until we got home for the penny to drop. At last he felt safe enough to collapse under his duvet, which he did for several days, shaking and crying with no food and little drink. He was wiped out and needed recovery time after contact with our alien world.

Hamish thinks that we would be more in tune with him if he was able to show his distress more obviously. His behaviours are too subtle for we mere mortals to pick up on without some expertise, an open heart, and a lot of time with Hamish. Fortunately, we have found a way to communicate together so that we can enable Hamish to tell us when he is struggling. Now that he is feeling more understood and, more importantly, that people really believe him, his anxiety levels are slowly lessening.

Until Hamish was diagnosed, he was not understood or believed. He was perceived as a highly sensitive, over-emotional child who was held back by an over-concerned and over-anxious mother! At school he presented very few problems. He was academically bright and he wore what we came to call his 'normal suit'. He used his large and learned repertoire of ways he had observed other people behave and speak. At home we were only too aware that something was wrong. It was here that he could download the stress he had endured during the day. There were hours of screaming, kicking or hurting the nearest person in sight. We began to think that we were going crazy and that we were hopelessly inadequate parents. We felt confused, isolated and started to doubt ourselves.

When Hamish was diagnosed, he was out of school so we actively started looking for somewhere that might match his needs. We looked into moving to Australia so that we could be around the expertise of Tony Attwood. In the end we set our sights on Sheffield and The Resource. We sold our house, found a job and moved. At first, Hamish was given an emergency placement at Bents Green (a wonderful special school), but later he was transferred to The Resource.

In Sheffield, we immediately found a palpable change in our mindset. It was the first time that we felt taken seriously and valued. Everything we said was believed and seemed useful. We were actively encouraged to be involved and respected as experts on our son. The more validated and appreciated we felt, the more our confidence grew and the more empowered we felt. As our confidence grew the better we became at reaching out to Hamish and at really beginning to understand him. The more we were believed, the more we were able to believe and be led by Hamish. When Hamish felt believed he was able to let us find ways to help him communicate with us. Empowering us, the parents, was a vitally potent part in the jigsaw of Hamish's growth. Once, when Hamish was really distressed and unable to get to school, Matthew told me to trust and follow my instincts about him. 'Do what you think is right for him.' How liberating was that sort of approach for us? It meant that as parents we could be so much more effective with our son. And Hamish – well he thrived on knowing that at last everyone was believing and trusting him.

Hamish is still severely disabled by his autism but has made enormous progress since his placement at Moorpark. This is a 52-week-a-year, 24-hours-a-day support placement and it is the first time in his life that he has experienced being in the right sort of sensory environment with committed and dedicated support. It has taken him a year at Moorpark to be soothed enough to begin his healing process. The staff are passionate to meet his needs and help him reach his potential. As a family, we have felt cherished by the care and understanding of Social Services, especially our two social workers, Pete and Katarina. We have been touched at how truly involved they have become and how much they have enjoyed getting to know Hamish and share in his successes.

It took a while for Hamish to come to terms with the fact that many of the other residents in the Moorpark community seem able to do far more than him even though they are non verbal and more obviously on the autistic spectrum. They are able to be sociable and to access more environments than him. However, now that he has his quiet, low sensory house, now that he feels so totally believed and that no one will rush him but follow his pace, he is feeling happier in his skin and is gradually stepping out. We can see that given the right ingredients of life, Hamish is making progress. We are all so proud of him. Meanwhile, he is proud to be Hamish and to be autistic saying that his autism is just part of him. Hamish is a worthy ambassador for autism, happy to tell anyone that he is autistic and what that means for him. To come to this place of comfort has taken a long while and has only come about since his time in The Resource. Hamish was not able to fully access the educational facilities of The Resource but what he did access was much more valuable. In The Resource under Matthew and the team, he was supported to take a difficult road of self-discovery, one that most adults will never dare to tread. He changed from being someone who felt raw and angry about his diagnosis, unable to accept that he was different from any other 'conventional' person, to being very happily autistic and willing to share his knowledge with us. Had he not taken that journey but continued with the façade of 'being normal', I think we would have lost him. The momentous energy he used to pretend that he was conventional would have dried up. But now, he can be his lovely self. That's what I call success. The spin off for us has been that we have been given a few enriching glimpses of Hamish's unique take on life – what an honour that has been.

CHAPTER 6

Supported Living

The Holy Grail

It seems right and proper to look at supported living in relation to people with ASDs after the previous chapter. Hamish is only one example of excellent supported living schemes. Not everyone needs a place such as Moorpark. The first two pupils who came to The Resource, Shaun and Andrew, are ready to leave home. I would imagine that there are times when their parents would like them to leave home. Sadly, nothing is that simple in terms of autism and supported living. The National Autistic Society has recently published a report about housing options for people with autism (Harker and King 2004). The title gives the game away quite early on *Tomorrow's Big Problem*. In her foreword, Dame Stephanie Shirley writes, 'Autistic Spectrum Disorders are generally overlooked when it comes to services' (p. 3). I am not sure this is strictly true. The disability of autism is certainly higher up on the agenda for social policy makers and officials from the health agencies than it was ten years ago. It is just that those people are not quite sure what to do with 'autism' when it does crop up on their agendas. It sometimes appears as if there are few professionals who actually know a little about autism at this policy making level of management, and certainly no one with an ASD. This excellent report highlights several cases where young people have had to move away from their local area because there are no other options, just like Hamish. This is far from ideal.

The professionals on the front line know that even the most academically gifted young adults are likely to have some impairment, or difference, with their social functioning. This 'difference', which runs through the very heart of autism, will impact in some way on an individual's ability to live independently. Support will be needed in getting and then managing a home. Clearly, this support will differ from person to person. This means that a diverse range of housing options and support needs to be available. This needs planning, investment, regular assessment and the political will to aim for the very best services. However it has to be accepted and acknowledged, that the 'most able' people with an ASD are likely to require an element of support with independent living in order to cope with the unexpected. At the moment (and I am sure Sheffield is not alone in this), the policy of 'muddling through' is proving expensive both in financial terms and to the individual and their families. For a worker on the front line, money has to be re-directed away from the issues of how to understand the causes of autism, into improving services to the people with autism themselves. In this respect, adult services undoubtedly need a huge injection of capital. Take the millions of pounds spent on research into causes and spend some of it on autism-specific supported living schemes.

Some of the glossy brochures coming out of various agencies in Sheffield at the moment centre on the latest (2004) Children Act from Parliament. They are littered with the exclamation, 'Every Child Matters' and five guiding values of: staying safe, staying healthy, enjoying and achieving, making a positive contribution and economic well-being. These principles and visions will be discussed at every level of local government agency involved in health, early years, education, leisure and social services. The leaders of these agencies are running 'road shows' where they will tell us all how things are going to change for the better for 0- to 19-year-olds in Sheffield. None of the principles, effort or determination behind this work can be questioned. It would end the class system in Britain and turn us all into a more equal nation of people. It sounds wonderful. It is part of the government's agenda to eradicate poverty and inequality. It is socialism in action, at least on paper.

Children's Centres will open where many of the services a parent might need for their offspring will be under one roof. Local people will be heavily involved in the establishment of these centres. Some of the investment will come from government, and some from lottery money. I am beginning to feel slightly dense because I am not sure where state funding ends and lottery funding starts. Our own lottery bid for supported employment was turned down, re-written and sent off again within three months of applying. Ironically, I seemed to get much more support and guidance from the lottery people once our bid had failed. Advice sheets with outcomes and criteria began to appear. This support would have been so much more useful at the start of the long process of filling in their bid forms. Re-writing the bid took up vast swathes of time. It is no wonder that the creativity of individuals is often beaten out of them by systems that have little room for flair, charisma, intuitive thinking and radical ideas. The future of our employment service rests on this lottery bid. This book will, I hope, be outdated in less time than it takes for our lottery money to run out. However, I digress.

The concept of enhanced funding and services for 0- to 19-year-olds is superb. However, in terms of autism, the funding gap is *after* the age of 19. It is a challenge to make a positive contribution or achieve economic well-being without a job. The heavy investment in services for people with ASDs is desperately needed in the 19 to old age bit of life. The words of our advocates reverberate from every corner of life – we are adults for a lot longer than we are children.

This sounds easy, and grounded in common sense. However, this concept is simplistic and has several fundamental flaws. When assessing the needs of a person, Social Services may have little problem with the fact that an ASD is life long and impairs social functioning. What causes a major problem is the concept of impaired intelligence. Some pupils at The Resource have measured intelligence quotients of well over 100. This discrimination on the basis of one measure of intelligence is a particular barrier to services for some people with Asperger's Syndrome. I return to the ridiculous notion that Social Services are deeming pupils in The Resource as young as 13 to be 'not disabled' on the basis of information written in a Statement.

The team of staff at The Resource and myself know that Shaun, Andrew and all our other friends will need some level of support when they leave home. For some, that may mean a couple of hours in the morning to make sure they are up, washed and dressed ready for work, and then a couple of hours in the evening to teach and support with living skills such as budgeting, shopping, cleaning and leisure activities. This might mean about twenty-five to thirty hours a week for maybe two to three years. Independence can grow within supported living just as it can do in a school or employment setting, especially if this is a seamless service from education to supported living and employment. Becoming increasingly independent is part of life for most people, however small the steps that are taken. This kind of service, which might be called 'floating support' would be delivered directly into the home of the person or people concerned. It is flexible. It could increase or decrease as appropriate. It cannot be delivered by people who have no training and are paid just above the minimum wage. It is a highly skilled job. Others may need a higher level of support with full-time staff living with three or four adults for maybe two to five years. After this length of time, and with experienced and skilled support, I would hope most of the young adults I know would be capable of moving onto a more independent lifestyle. Some level of support will always be needed by each person I know, even if that is a monthly meeting to check if things are all right.

I have done my level best to make sense of the Department of Health Guidelines to local authorities on setting criteria for adult social care (implemented April 2003). First, I felt the need to do a Masters degree in English because the guidelines are about as easy to read and interpret as *Macbeth* would be if Shakespeare had written it while under the influence of strong hallucinogenic drugs. There are some wonderful statements that made my heart soar like, 'Councils should make changes in their practice to take a longer-term preventative view of individuals' needs and circumstances.' I love the phrase 'longer term'. It breeds hope and the idea that someone somewhere is looking farther than their next budget planning meeting. The basis of the guidelines is that there should be four bands of need when assessing the social care needs of an individual: critical, substantial, moderate and low. However, the best piece of guidance for councils is: should people be helped or not?

Within these four eligibility bands, there are some good-sounding bits, and some not-so-good bits. A lovely fact according to these guidelines is that councils should not only identify immediate needs, but also needs that would worsen if support was not given. The factor that appears to work against a lot of people with ASDs centres on the issues of personal care and domestic routines. To gain consideration for a critical level of need in this area, a person has to have an inability to carry out vital personal care or domestic routines. To gain acceptance of a substantial need, a person has to have an inability to carry out the majority of personal care or domestic routines. An inability to carry out several personal care or domestic routines gains a person a moderate level of need. You can probably predict what constitutes a low level of need – an inability to carry out one or two personal care or domestic routines. It is precisely this kind of nonsensical criteria that ensure too many people on the spectrum remain living at home with parents or carers.

In a study published in 2001, J. Barnard *et al.* found that 57 per cent of adults aged over 16 were living with their family. For those aged over 25, the figure only fell to 44 per cent. In a report from the NAS in 2003 (*Autism: Rights in Reality*), Steve Broach (*et al.*) point out that 'more adults with autistic spectrum disorders live in the family home than in any other setting, while progress towards supported living and away from residential settings remains slow' (p.20).

Meanwhile, still in the real world, and very much a part of those stark statistics, Shaun, Andrew and our other friends have, to some extent, become victims of their own success and that of the service they have received up to the age of 19. This complicates and muddies an already bleak picture in terms of them gaining some support with independent living. These young adults are more than able to carry out the physical tasks involved in personal care and domestic routines. They will not need physical help in and out of the bath, or support with brushing their teeth. However, they may need verbal or visual prompting to see to their personal hygiene needs. Most of these young adults are capable of learning how to use public transport, and it is to be hoped that the majority will have jobs. When this is coupled to the fact that their IQ is generally above 70, they are unlikely to access the levels of funding needed in order to finance adequate supported living schemes, even if such schemes existed. The fact that a person with an ASD may have an IQ of over 70, and they have learnt to look after themselves after years of training and teaching, appears to rule them out of a system that is undoubtedly in crisis.

As the NAS report, *Tomorrow's Big Problem* (Harker and King 2004) points out '...assessments should be carried out but a concern for those with autistic spectrum disorders is that eligibility for services may be a problem for those who are thought not to have a learning disability or do not fit the higher risk categories' (p.26). The awkwardness of this situation seems to leave councils in limbo in determining who has critical needs in terms of provision of services. A more cynical person might argue that, for some people with ASDs, it gives councils a 'legitimate' way out.

I can see the problems with budgets and demands for services that local government agencies like Social Services are under. They face a potentially endless demand for services and their pot of money is limited. Supported living has to be rationed in some way, and it is those who appear to have the greatest needs that gain the highest levels of support. In this case, large numbers of people with ASDs will miss out. Put yourself in the position of a social worker faced with a high functioning adult with an ASD whose difficulties are hidden by good verbal skills. That social worker may have to assess the housing and support needs of the person. What chance do they stand of getting it right, even if the resources needed were available?

We have an accommodation plan here in Sheffield. Autism is rarely mentioned within this plan. There are simply too many other demands for services from other areas. I was privileged when the person who wrote this accommodation plan accepted my invitation to come and have a meeting at The Resource. She listened carefully to our ideas and frustrations. When she told me about the challenges the various agencies involved are facing, I have to admit to initially being stunned into silence. In Sheffield alone, there are over 300 individuals with some form of recognised disability who are living at home with parents or carers who themselves, are aged 70 or over. Some of these individuals will be people on the spectrum. As a human being, presented with that cold hard fact, I had little to say to her in reply. I commiserated with her and made some more tea. The issues I felt strongly about, like Shaun and Andrew having a good supported living scheme at the age of 20, just faded away.

However, once I had got over the trauma and probable human cost of these figures, common sense started to kick back in with renewed vigour. To begin with, if the support that these individuals and families have received has been in some way inadequate, there is a great likelihood of some 'spillage' over into mental health problems. Barnard *et al.* (2001) found 32 per cent of families in a survey reported mental health issues as a problem. That is not acceptable and it must be hugely expensive. It may also lead people with autism into mental health services. This could be disastrous if only the 'presented needs' are addressed. Presumably, at some point, each of these 300 or more individuals in Sheffield will have some kind of crisis. At some point, their parents or carers will die. For parents and carers, there is no way round the question, 'what will happen to them when we die'? I can only imagine that this figure will rise considerably over the next ten years. Social Services will then have to step in and deal with the situation. They will have to provide some level of service. In fact, it seems that social services are quite used to dealing with 'crisis points'. In many respects, the four levels of need outlined in this chapter are still based on the needs of elderly people when they have to be taken into residential or nursing homes.

What our service to teenagers and young people with ASDs has at the moment is no crisis point. There are plenty of questions without answers, but no major disasters. However, that is not to say that there will be zero challenges in the future. I guarantee that some of my friends will hit crisis points in the future. The stark alternative (or reality) is that the majority of my friends will continue to live at home, with aging parents, or that the level of service they receive will be directly linked to the wealth of their parents. For social services to get involved now for the 19- to 25-year-olds, and provide the necessary range of quality supported living schemes, would in the long run, be far more cost-effective than waiting for, and responding to, crisis points. A crisis by its very nature is expensive and distressing. What is needed in 'politician's speak' is a seamless service for people with ASDs from cradle to grave, a kind of 'resource' for life that a person can dip into and out of when needed, or necessary. We have to keep posing the question, to anyone who will listen: what happens to our friends aged over 19 after society has invested all this money and effort in education, independence training and employment, if we have nothing suitable to follow it up with? I am confident that our government, just like the wonderful person who wrote Sheffield's accommodation plan, is worried about people living with parents or carers aged 70 and over. Deeming a pupil aged 14 to be 'not disabled' does not help. We should be entering into a discussion about future living needs when a pupil is 14 years old so that parents can plan for the future in plenty of time. Plans are of little use if a range of supported living schemes are either non-existent, or of a poor quality. Quality can always be improved by involving people who have a good understanding and experience of autistic spectrum disorders. It could be improved further by the involvement of people with an ASD. We waste so much human talent.

We realised that our small charity would never be able to manage quality supported living schemes, even if there were changes in the eligibility criteria that encouraged a more forward looking model for the distribution of funds. Several years ago we forged a partnership with an excellent provider of supported living schemes in the UK – The Disabilities Trust. It was an exciting time. The Consultant Psychiatrist in Learning Disabilities for The Disabilities Trust (an excellent woman who taught me so much) travelled around Sheffield visiting some of my friends. I introduced this wonderful woman to nine young adults and their families and she then wrote a report about their support needs as an adult. These reports were sent to Social Services, as we had nothing to hide. For a few brief hours, it actually felt as if we were making a difference. A service manager from The Disabilities Trust attended a public meeting with parents in Sheffield and told them to 'dream big'.

Eddie was one such person whom we interviewed in order to assess his support needs. His parents were also consulted and fully involved. The report from The Disabilities Trust states that in many respects, Eddie is very able. He wants to be seen as intelligent and independent. However, Eddie can be neglectful of his personal care if not prompted (he only needs prompting to attend to his personal care needs, not physical 'hands-on' support). Eddie did not want or need a full-time member of staff living in the same house, although he acknowledged that he had a lot to learn about looking after himself.

Eddie is emotionally vulnerable and has already had brief associations with youths who could lead him into major trouble. Eddie may not fully understand these social situations. The report concludes by stating that Eddie needs an environment where his adult domestic and self-care skills are developed in a systematic and structured way. The atmosphere generated by this supported living environment must be calm and respectful. Eddie must have opportunities to talk about how he relates to other people and to feel absolutely safe in doing so. His vocational training is going well and must be protected (Eddie had gained a number of paid hours work in a large department store in the city centre having done work experience there while at The Resource and at college). His leisure interests could be developed too. There was nothing radical about this report.

I did not write this report about Eddie's needs. An expert in the field who had met Eddie on two separate occasions wrote it. This woman personified the idea that: knowledge speaks, but wisdom listens. I read her report and was delighted by the insight she had shown. This was an expert saying it the way it was for Eddie at that time. Nine such reports were written, probably at great expense to The Disabilities Trust. They were all grounded in common sense and a practical approach to support needs for a smooth transition into adult life. Had they been acted on, some of those nine young people would now be moving onto a more independent way of living with their self-esteem intact. (Only one of these nine young adults is receiving excellent support. To achieve this, his parents had to challenge the eligibility criteria and the social service assessments.) Their practical life skills would have been grounded in real life situations. Staff experienced and knowledgeable about ASDs would have delivered their support. After the reports from The Disabilities Trust came the social service assessments of need. Perhaps because the disability of autism is relatively new in terms of distinct features and understanding, it has undoubtedly lagged behind other disabilities in the provision of services from health, education and adult services.

For the reasons outlined in the NAS report on housing options, these young adults did not meet the usual service definitions of need. It became clear that the services were (and still are) some way behind in their thinking and ability to respond. With hindsight, I do not

believe we could have done any more to help Social Services understand what we were trying to achieve, and what needed to be put in
place in terms of a range of housing services. Two of the excellent
social workers involved in assessing these young adults spent time at
The Resource to improve their own understanding of autism and the
complex individual needs. They willingly went the extra mile. The
problems involved in the issues of supported living rarely come down
to inadequate or obstructive individual workers, rather the restrictive,
inappropriate and totally under-funded systems within which they
have to operate. These individual social workers may have had a case-
load of up to 150 adults in need. It is not difficult to imagine that the
300 or so disabled people in Sheffield who currently live with parents or carers who are aged over 70 will double and possibly treble
over the next five to ten years unless investment occurs at an earlier
stage of life.

I recently met a lovely educational psychologist in Surrey. This is
an area of England that has a high percentage of children in private
education (one in five) and this reflects a high level of personal wealth
in this beautiful part of the country. He was knowledgeable about our
work in Sheffield, but remained totally opposed to opening integrated resources for pupils with ASD in primary or secondary
schools. His attitude was that all schools should be able to manage
pupils with ASDs effectively, and be flexible enough in their
approaches to learning and the curriculum. In effect, he was espous-
ing the values inherent in 'every child matters'. I also met the three
superb teachers who acted as advisors to primary and secondary
schools in this large area of the country. Their attitude was very different to that of the educational psychologist. They were doing their
best to support an ever-increasing number of pupils in the public and
private sector, but felt that on occasions, their messages and training
were falling short. They could troubleshoot, advise and enable, but
then inevitably had to move onto the next school and the next crisis.
The psychologist assured me that more money would go into
expanding this team of three staff. The money would probably be
better spent on buying a helicopter to reduce the amount of travelling
time of the current team.

This educational psychologist was being far more idealistic than I am sometimes accused of being if he thinks all schools will make a concerted effort to be more 'autism friendly'. There are too many other pressures on schools to make the necessary changes in order to benefit pupils with ASDs. There has to be a bigger and more supportive 'kick' to achieve change of this kind. A visit from an autism advisory teacher once a week for six weeks will rarely be enough. The teacher knows it and so do the schools. There has to be a bigger and more supportive 'kick' to initiate and then guide social service investment in a range of supported living schemes for adults with ASDs.

Eddie, who was 20 at this point, had a crisis soon after being assessed by Social Services. A well-meaning professional had told Eddie's mother that he would never be seen as a priority in terms of housing unless there was a crisis, preferably involving the police. Probably for that reason, and a whole bundle of other related pressures and stresses, Eddie and his mother fell out, the police were called and they arrested him for assault. After a few hours in a police cell, and lengthy interviews, Eddie was cautioned. He was provided with a volunteer legal support worker (who had received some training on autism). This person did not know Eddie, and I can imagine that it would have been a tough task to interpret, advise and guide him through this traumatic experience. Eddie's father arrived as soon as possible, considering that his partner was giving birth to their first child.

With no autism specific supported living schemes available (or in existence), Eddie ended up in a residential home for adults with learning disabilities. The staff at this home were caring, professional and willing to help Eddie, but he did not want to be there. He hated it. Eddie does not see himself as learning disabled. He views himself as someone who has Asperger's Syndrome. To eat, share space and sleep near people whom Eddie considered disabled was more than he could stand. A further incident in the home saw Eddie moved to a different residential provision for adults with learning disabilities. Throughout this traumatic period of Eddie's life, his father was working behind the scenes to secure him an opportunity for independent living with some level of support. This should not have been a battle. Provisions should have already been in place. Throughout this period of six months, Eddie did well to keep his job in a department store in the city centre. However, it is fair to say that the trauma involved severely threatened his successful employment.

To help this situation, we talked to Eddie's manager at work to enable him to understand what was happening. To his credit, this manager was extremely supportive, and did his best to understand, and make allowances when Eddie was late for work, or just did not turn up.

Social Services, working with a housing association found Eddie a flat. I have a vivid memory of receiving a call from Eddie and him telling me that he was scared and lonely. It was only after a few minutes that I realised it was his first night alone in this flat. A few nights later, Eddie phoned to tell me about a neighbour who had threatened to kill him. Eddie was worried about safety and security and so had checked the door was locked several times by opening it, closing it, and locking it securely. The noise of this echoing round the corridors must have been quite loud. The repetition had annoyed Eddie's neighbour, and the 'threat' was made. All I could do was re-assure Eddie that this was an idle threat, but that he should not check the door anymore. Once I put the phone down, all I could do was hope that this was a correct assessment of the situation. Sometimes my wife accuses me of being unable to 'switch off'. However, if Eddie phones, she is understanding and patient. It is easy to see that there are times and situations in which Eddie is totally vulnerable.

Social Services through careful assessments deemed that Eddie needed seven hours a week support. It is not enough. Having achieved this level of support, I know other parents who dare not complain because they fear that even this paltry level of support could be reduced or withdrawn. When Eddie has run out of money, wants advice on washing or ironing, feels threatened by a neighbour, or simply needs someone to talk through his latest worries (which are many), the chances are it will be in one of the other 161 hours in a week. Put yourself in Eddie's shoes. What would you do if your anxiety levels were going through the roof? You would be likely to turn to a trusted friend. At these times, Eddie will phone his father, or me. There are some weeks when Eddie does not phone me at work or home and I have to assume that things are all right. There are some weeks when there will be several calls in one evening from Eddie, usually with the request, 'can you call me back because I don't have any credit on my mobile'.

Eddie likes to go out at night and have a good time. He is probably drinking a little too much. He certainly gives too much money to the 'oldest profession in the world' and then has endless worries about it. He lends money to people he sees as 'friends' and then (understandably) gets cross when they do not pay him back. A few neighbours have certainly taken advantage of Eddie's naivety. To balance this out, one neighbour has been extremely supportive and protective towards Eddie. However, this should not cloud the central issues. Eddie is surviving…just. He should be a success story. There are times when I feel that 'the crisis' is imminent. I have every faith that Social Services will step in if/when this crisis happens and save the day. However, they do not have a range of provisions that are autism specific, and if they did, there would be no need for them to save the day in the first place.

Given autism specific support in the right quantity, Eddie could successfully manage with seven hours a week support in two to three years' time. The crisis, should it happen, will be far more expensive than providing two years of the right quality and level of support for Eddie now. What he needs now is continued structured support with shopping, washing, ironing, budgeting, staying safe, risk taking, leisure activities, making future plans, time management, and more work on friendships and relationships. If/when a crisis happens, the chances of Eddie losing his paid employment will be high. His opportunities to continue to learn and grow through inclusion in society will be potentially lost. His fellow employees will see somebody with autism who ultimately did not quite make it. Perhaps some of them will console themselves by saying things like, 'oh well, at least he'll be well looked after now'. Eddie would no longer be contributing to their knowledge and understanding of autism. Work will be undone, self-esteem will suffer, investment will be wasted and the financial costs will be greater. Eddie could (quite rightly) be claiming higher levels of state benefit and no longer paying tax. What a waste of talent, time, resources and energy.

Eddie would benefit from continued work with a communication therapist as an adult. Two such people visited The Resource to see if the health authority could do anything to support some of these young adults like Eddie. I was faced with two brilliant people who yet again, wanted to help. Access to communication therapy is very similar to the situation with supported living. Eddie has an IQ of above 70 and so he cannot have access to any kind of service from adult communication therapy. It is easy to become demoralised in all this whether a parent or a professional. I always become frustrated when some of our critics claim that our service takes 'more able' pupils and adults with ASDs. What defines ability and disability should be a dead-end of a debate. In reality, Eddie's problems centre on an IQ level that is above 70. This disables him far more than his autism ever could.

As usual, I find myself short on answers. Autism is a specialist area of work, and services, when they are more universally provided, need to be managed and run by people who know what they are talking about. This is not meant to sound arrogant in any way. If I have a problem with my achilles tendon that requires surgery, I expect the operation to be carried out by an orthopaedic surgeon and a skilled team in this area of medicine. People with ASDs have every right to expect their support, guidance and learning for life to be carried out by staff who are skilled, knowledgeable and experienced in this specialised area of work. With the best will in the world, people with little or no experience of working with people on the spectrum can often do more harm than good. We should not be surprised by that, it is just that sometimes we forget to place enough emphasis on the nitty gritty issues. We also forget to say the obvious, in case we somehow upset other people.

The hidden nature of autism held back services in early years and education for too long. We are now seeing the same effect holding back the provision of a range of supported living schemes for people with ASDs. The social housing sector has (rightly) placed great emphasis on meeting the very obvious needs of people with physical disabilities. Now we have to push for ASDs within this complex area that is so starved of funds. However, nobody is holding out 'the begging bowl' because there is no need. 'Cost' and 'investment' are two completely different things. Compared to residential living, support for a large number of people with an ASD to live independently or semi-independently is low cost. The investment in skilled support will actually be cost effective and in the long run, save money.

With adequate investment and planning now, there should be no need for housing to be 'tomorrow's big problem'. For those professionals in the field, common sense has to be at the forefront of any improvements in investment that might be achieved over the next few years. A range of housing options always comes at the top of the list. People on the spectrum have particular and very individual needs, and services must be able to respond in flexible and innovative ways. All services in health, education, mainstream and mental health departments need to give particular attention to those people whose needs are centred on the autistic spectrum. There are immense training issues and needs. Anoraks have to find greater access to people in these services who, through no fault of their own, know little about ASDs. Politely knocking on their doors may not be enough.

People with ASDs need to be considered and included in the decisions about supported living schemes that are being taken at executive level now. Parents need to challenge decisions based on inappropriate eligibility criteria through appeal to the highest possible level. However, there must be a better way forward than individual battles. There is little use in excluding all of those adults on the spectrum with IQs of over 70 (unless there is a crisis involving the police). Decisions based on that kind of misunderstanding do not belong in the twenty-first century, and friends like Eddie, deserve and need so much more.

CHAPTER 7

There May Be Trouble Ahead

People who visit The Resource quickly realise that I get a tremendous kick out of coming to work each day. Visiting parents are booked in for a half-hour slot. My wonderful colleague, Lucy can usually stick to this. Parents who end up with me are usually in for an hour or so. Visiting professionals now pay for their visits so I do not have to feel as guilty for the time it takes up (and these visits earn about £1200 each year for our charity.) Whether it is the pupils, parents, or visiting professionals, I know I am going to learn something new. That is a privileged position to be in. The team I work alongside has had no one leave for over three years. New staff have been added as we have gained more pupils, and these additions have been superb. Staff have a yearly 'supervision' meeting with either Lucy or me. These are brilliant sessions for me to catch up with how a member of the team is feeling. They also give me an opportunity to say 'thank you.'

The hostility we felt in this mainstream secondary school towards us and our work no longer exists. Most of it came from a fear of the unknown. There was no reason to expect a smooth ride. Staff from The Resource and mainstream staff had to grow and learn together. Although this is still ongoing, mainstream staff new to the school are now expected to attend training about autism and The Resource. We have had to employ a variety of strategies for gently removing any barriers which people may have put in our way. There can be a cost to this process and I can well understand other specialist resources in the UK that have had more time than us to prepare, experiencing severe challenges. Staff working in these specialist provisions can be under enormous pressure. There was no easy ride here for the first five years. We never felt secure. I have made myself unpopular in some quarters over the last eleven years. Our work always appears to be received better outside of Sheffield than within the city boundaries. That remains a source of personal sadness. Staff have not been allowed anywhere near the other two autism resources that have been established in secondary schools in Sheffield. Our role in pushing back the boundaries is not recognised, and the expertise of staff at The Resource is not utilised. What a waste of talent and experience. The very least we should have been invited to do, was share all the mistakes we have made. I have not done anything about this situation. Sometimes it has been necessary to stand and fight, and sometimes it is best to bite your tongue and run for cover. Cover is good. Local Education Authorities (or whatever will replace them) tend to be run by people who have forgotten what it is like to work on the front line. That happens and it is not their fault. Their priorities are different from yours and mine.

I still try to think up theories and philosophies that can explain what has happened at King Ecgbert School over the past eleven years. Most days, I still do not believe how well the pupils are doing myself. As the reader may have guessed by now, theory is not my strong suit. It is so much easier to devise a set of principles or values after good practices have developed or evolved. The academic community has led us to believe that this is, in some way, cheating. However, it seems to me that to start with a theory, vision, or set of values seems to reduce creativity, innovation and common sense. Part of me wishes that the following ten factors were written in tablets of stone before we started our work. These are the guiding principles which appear to underpin our work in access and inclusion for pupils on the autistic spectrum:

1. individual needs-led approach

2. a belief and focus on the strengths of individuals with an ASD

3. naivety

4. common sense

5. a basic understanding of the current thinking about autism

6. the continual need to ask questions

7. a desire to change things for the better

8. an openness about autism with anyone who will listen

9. never thinking we were experts, but, it is to be hoped, part of any possible solutions

10. a willingness to work in partnerships.

Approaches to autism have to be individual because the more I learn, the more I think people on the spectrum are more individual than non-autistic people. Two of our current Y10 pupils (aged 15 years old) have 'fled the nest'. They no longer want to be seen as being part of The Resource. They have (through negotiation during their first two years) decided on a full timetable in mainstream. They want no visible support in lessons. Both have had counselling about their autism and what it means to them. Academically, they are average or above average pupils, and have opted for no extra time in formal exams. Occasionally they might ask for a bit of help with something, or one of their teachers will ask me to chase up a missing piece of work. We were able to arrange suitable placements for them during their two-week block of work experience. Another friend of mine needs much closer support and contact with staff from The Resource. He celebrates his Asperger's Syndrome and does not believe in making too many concessions towards other people. He is who he is, take him or leave him. There are twenty-eight pupils supported by staff from The Resource and there are twenty-eight different curricula and approaches. With the 'adequate staffing ratio' declared by OFSTED, we should not find that unusual or radical.

One of our young Y7 pupils (aged 12) struggles to see his strengths. He finds academic work a real challenge, but has increasingly shown great determination to succeed. He finds it difficult to do homework at home and so gets into bother for missing pieces of work. His attendance at school was not as good as it should have been when he first started in his Y7. Gradually, he has seen some rewards for the increased effort he has put in. He was nominated for an award at the school's achievement evening. I was lucky enough to see him go to the front and receive his certificate. It was a proud evening for him and his parents. He did a great poem in English. When he saw that this had been put on our website (www.kesresource.org.uk), he bristled with pride although he announced quite forcibly, that he did not want to be famous. His attendance has improved and he is so much more positive in his attitude and outlook. It is not difficult to see or play to individual strengths within autism. They are as many and as varied as the people themselves.

Alastair scraped through his A Levels a couple of years ago. This was remarkable since he lost all interest in Maths and Physics very early on in his advanced studies. His desire was to go to university to study IT and computer generated music. He enrolled on a Music A Level course at college first but it did not work out well. We went out for a drink together six months ago, and he told me about his band and how they had produced two CDs of their music. These were being marketed though a website he had designed. He considered that his Asperger's Syndrome was now very much secondary to who he was. As I listened to this articulate, thoughtful, calm and honest young man, I could not disagree with his opinion. His aim was to arrange some gigs for his band so that they could perform live. This was a huge undertaking and Alastair was understandably nervous about the prospect of performing in public. He did not want me to attend the first gig because he saw it as a kind of practice to iron out any difficulties. However, he did telephone me to tell me about this first gig. There were some mistakes but his band and four others played in front of about 150 people. The second gig will be in a couple of months, and I am invited to this one. I have offered to sell the CDs and T-shirts. Where this journey will take Alastair, I am not sure. However, he is doing something he loves and no one can argue with that.

In this line of work, there are times when staff cannot help but be naive. Jonathon wanted to have a weekly work placement in a local post office during his Y9 (when he was 14 years old). We went to the post office to talk to the manager. She was hesitant and took some time to think about whether it was a good idea or not. A member of staff took Jonathon to meet her, and we gave her some literature to read. Several weeks went past before she phoned to say that it was a great idea and she would love to offer Jonathon a weekly placement. He quickly became independent on the placement and it lasted for one year. The only reason it stopped was because there was simply not enough work for him to do. There should not be any barriers to us asking for a break, however uncomfortable it might be. We have to believe (however naively) that every time we ask for a chance for an individual pupil, the answer is going to be yes. For the next academic year, staff have made visits to request placements at two garden centres, another post office, a supermarket not yet involved in our scheme, a fruit shop, a café, and a small garage. If all of these placements turned into reality, we would be able to offer the three pupils who need them a bit of choice.

None of our ten guiding principles are anything special. The vision of 'every child matters' is nothing special. What makes a vision special is how the aspects of it are put into practice. If the name of a pupil has been omitted from the programme for an achievement evening, it is vital that it is reprinted correctly. If staff feel that more than one adult needs to support a number of pupils on an out of school event, then that has to happen. Not all staff from The Resource can get on well with all of our mainstream colleagues. It makes sense to accept this and then play to strengths within the team. If I struggle to see many strengths in a particular colleague from mainstream, then why should I have to support pupils in his/her lesson? It makes more sense for someone else to take on this support. Within the team, I am lucky to have staff who actually like English, History, Technology, Maths, Art, Sociology and Science. These same people will express fear and trepidation if they have too many lessons in a subject where they feel less comfortable. As far as possible, it is common sense to play to people's strengths. People will always work harder if they are happy in their jobs. Towards the end of an academic year, the more I see my colleagues sitting in The Resource drinking coffee and chatting to each other, the happier I am. They would not be doing this unless they had done a brilliant job in meeting the support needs of the pupils they work alongside. This is still something I would not readily talk about with an LEA inspector because I doubt they would understand. Staff know that at the beginning of an academic year, there will be no sitting round chatting for anyone. Visitors are not permitted at The Resource until after the first half term in October, because all staff are on full contact timetables.

When Jonathon's placement at the post office was ended after one year because there was not enough work, we had to say, 'thanks, it's been great, and Jonathon has loved it'. What we cannot say is, 'come on, not enough work, pull the other one it's got bells on it'. It is not the time to draw a line in the sand and call their bluff. The fact is, the manager of the post office and her employee have done a great job with Jonathon over twelve months. They may feel as though they have 'done their bit'. They have certainly done more than most and we are grateful for their involvement. It is time to move on and find Jonathon a new placement. He knows this and does not have a problem with it. Common sense has to be the strongest principle pulsing though every vein of a public service.

To gain a basic understanding of autism and the current thinking and theories, the first point of call always has to be the young people with autism themselves. Given space, time and staff who listen, they will be our best teachers about their differences. Parents can be a huge asset as active partners. The detail provided by some parents about the previous eleven years of their son/daughter's life can help us provide the right kind of support and structure for that individual. We have held three conferences about our work in access and inclusion. It is an honour to have so many people who want to come and learn about our work. However, the importance of these days for me and other staff is that we get to hear some wonderful speakers. We always book someone who is on the spectrum to talk about their life and their experiences. There is always a parent who will talk about their experiences as well. Last year we were lucky enough to have Luke and Jacqui Jackson. It is always a great privilege to listen to Ros Blackburn or Richard Exley. Experts in the field such as Digby Tantum and Tony Attwood will always add to our current thinking and practice. Books about autism no longer fit on just one table at conferences.

Some of my colleagues went to listen to John Clements who is a brilliant Clinical Psychologist and behaviour consultant. They returned to work the next day full of smiles and renewed confidence. At our next department meeting, they had the opportunity to tell us all what they had learnt and how it could affect future practices. The overriding feeling that they had left with was that we were doing all right. Although they had not heard anything startling from John in terms of new and innovative thinking, what he had given them was a sense that our high expectations, the way we operate alongside parents, and the way in which our pupils are active participants in their learning was all correct and that these approaches would reap dividends. He had offered no grand prescriptive 'answers' because they do not exist. But, he had made people doing a good job, feel proud about what they do. Given support, togetherness and a good working environment, people can move mountains. My colleagues left this excellent training feeling that the next battle was worth it, and that their thinking and efforts were on the right lines.

Sometimes, when I walk into our area of the school, it seems like pupils and staff are waiting for me. If I am tired, the questions appear endless and answers are needed instantly. With the sheer number of decisions staff have to take each day, it is not surprising that mistakes are made. However, I would much rather the questions keep flowing. They are a perfect sign that staff are thinking ahead, questioning previously held thoughts and ideas, and thinking about their own practice. Department meetings are a great opportunity to discuss individual children and approaches. Our meetings are often lively affairs with a large dose of laughter thrown in for good measure. My life would be better if certain pupils would not question me about where the school purchasing catalogue is, or whether I use any products to stop me going bald. But then, maybe their lives would not be as good if they did not feel comfortable enough to ask these repetitive questions in the first place. At least they ask at lunchtime and not usually in the middle of a Maths lesson. But, you can never be sure of that!

A desire to change things for the better for people with ASDs is not difficult because there is simply so much to do. The disability is so far behind other kinds of additional needs such as Down's Syndrome.

The complexity of autism means that it is work on the front line with individuals that will make the biggest difference. We have to prepare the Andrews, Toms, Johns, Hannahs and Lees to be 'out there' in the world of work so that they can become the teachers for their fellow workers and managers. The large absence of people with ASDs in the mainstream of our society means that other people simply do not have to learn.

Glynis has a strong desire to change things for the better at Meadowhall. Lee, who had a Christmas job at Marks and Spencer has a strong desire to change things for the better. He has recently re-gained his job at Marks and Spencer for the summer period when many employees take their annual leave. He did not have to go through the interview process. They promised him a job when a suitable vacancy arose. At a recent social night out at a pub in town, Lee walked in looking visibly taller. He bristled with pride as he told friends about his start date and how he hoped this would change from a summer job, into a Christmas job, and then become a more permanent position. I do not think that Marks and Spencer will need any prompting to make his dream come true. All the young adults are proud of themselves, and each other. Others, who are on work placements, aspire to get that first paid position.

So many parents visit The Resource saying that they are less interested in academic success for their son or daughter, and much more concerned with them simply being happy, calm and 'in control' people who will have something to contribute to society. It does not seem too much to ask, but the practicalities of achieving such results must never be underestimated. When John became upset at work in the kitchen of a busy restaurant when a fellow employee changed the radio channel that was his favourite, Glynis had a lot of work to do with him and his colleagues. John needs to learn that he cannot always listen to his favourite radio station, and his colleagues have to recognise how important this station is in his life. Changing things for the better is just another learning experience in life's rich and varied tapestry. Understanding has to be encouraged and enhanced on both sides.

These kinds of opportunities give anoraks the chance to talk to people who really matter – the vast majority of people who know little or nothing about autism. As Richard Exley says, they are opportunities to 'take the dis out of disability'. Once John's employees realised how precious this one radio station is to him, it is not a great hardship for them to listen to it while he is in work. They can listen to other radio stations when he is not on duty. Unless someone is very immature or malicious, they are not going to disagree with this reasoning or common sense. When they meet other people and talk about work, they may mention John, his autism, and how he likes to listen to a particular radio station. I would hope they also comment on how hard he works, his excellent punctuality and faultless attendance. Setting off 'chain reactions' of this type will raise awareness and understanding. The trigger for this raising of awareness is the fact that John is in work in the first place.

One of our young Y11 pupils wants to work as a car mechanic. He has had two years' work experience in a car showroom, but he is bored with this as it is mainly cleaning cars. I went to see the manager of a small garage near to the school that would be perfect for this lad to gain more hands-on experience. The manager was out, but I managed to get his wife talking about the garage. We had a long chat about autism, this particular lad, and the work that we had done over the years. She was really interested but said that her husband was less sympathetic about 'these things'. I left her some newspaper articles about our work and our website address. She phoned a few days later to tell me she had not forgotten, and had decided to wait until her husband was in a good mood before she put the idea to him. I am sure she will be far more effective with her husband than I could have been. If this placement happens, it will be down to the manager being out when I called. The placement's success will then be down to the Y11 pupil. He should be fine because he wants to enrol for a car maintenance course at college once he leaves school.

There are no experts in The Resource other than the pupils themselves. There are many times when staff are faced with tough decisions about how to handle a situation or incident. The children in The Resource need structure, routine, adults whom they can trust and they also need to have some fun whenever possible. However, I am not sure how we measure expertise or how often we actually get a situation right. Perfect days at school, can mean horrendous nights at home. We see the children for about 190 days a year in neat six-and-a-half hour blocks at a time. With twenty-eight pupils, there are no smooth days anymore, nor should they be expected. How far staff can 'step into the shoes' of a pupil differs on a case-by-case basis. Supportive parents make this so much easier to do, but I do not have to experience the potentially horrendous nights at home with someone on the spectrum.

When the phone rings and it is a parent of someone in another school, in a different part of the country, and they are at their wits' end because of the situation breaking down at their son or daughter's school, all I can do is listen. Advice is limited and generalisations are to be avoided. If any of the pupils at The Resource are experiencing issues that are outside our limited knowledge, I should be able to turn for outside help. There are times when parents clutch at straws, and there are times when I do the same. Autism is as complex as human nature itself and people in the field (including parents) can only do their best.

For this reason, working in partnerships is vital. There are no short cuts to this because partnerships are about mutual learning, compromise and utilising all possible strength areas. It can take a little time for some of our mainstream colleagues to view Resource staff as anything more than 'helpers'. I do believe that the majority of our pupils gain strength from each other and the staff with whom they work. They gain strength from some sense of shared ownership of autism. The vast majority of pupils in The Resource know about their ASD and ask questions as and when they feel the need. This journey of self-discovery is facilitated by staff who are more than willing to travel alongside. There are the inevitable conflicts, but no one with an ASD is alone. There is support and celebration of each other's achievements. The school we work within has proved to be an excellent educational partner. Autism, and the individuals within The Resource are appreciated and increasingly understood. It is accepted that staff will argue from a child-centred point of view. It is equally accepted by staff in The Resource that sometimes, it is just impossible (in the short run) to change a situation to suit individual need.

Our partnership with Sheffield College (the major post-16 provider in the city) has been weakened by key personnel leaving the service. Changes are still being made, but this has meant a closer look at alternative post-16 providers. However, compared to the situation ten years ago, there appears to be an increasing awareness of autism within post-16 providers. There are simply more anoraks out there than ever before.

The employers with whom we have gone into partnership have been kind, open and willing to learn. However, partnerships have to be reciprocal in some way. Employers are not fools. It is no coincidence that initially, many of Andrew's shifts at Sainsbury's were over the lunchtime period (10 a.m. – 2 p.m.) which was a time when a lot of the workers who were doing a regular eight-hour shift were on their break. However, you never heard Andrew (or us) complain.

All this sounds very optimistic. However, there has been a cost to providing our ever-expanding service over the past eleven years. The cost, as usual within a public service, is a very human one.

We could not run our supported employment service without the backing of a charity. Staff and parents had to establish this charity and it is managed in our spare time. At the time of writing, we had enough money to continue to pay Glynis's salary for nine months. There was still no news on our re-submitted lottery bid. After that date, we would be quite literally, broke. In some ways, writing this book has taken my mind away from this simple and stark fact. Children, teenagers and adults with ASDs require support. This support requires investment. Plans have to be in place to avoid the many horror stories we all know and hear about. I am certain that this investment in people should not be largely based on money raised by charities.

The year 2002 in the UK was Autism Awareness Year. It was heralded with great fanfares and a small fortune spent on glossy brochures and empty promises. Nothing appeared to change except for a few mission statements from politicians printed on expensive paper. I actually dreaded the following plain old year of 2003. We have had visits from local Members of Parliament and a high-ranking Minister from the Department of Health. Nobody has contacted me to say

> now then Mr Matthew, we know you and your team have done a first rate job over the past few years, and we recognise that part of this work has been financed through charitable means. We also

know that this service will save us some money, so here is some state funding of £25,000 a year for the next five years. Stop wasting time raising the money yourselves and plough all your energies into being increasingly successful with the people your team works alongside.

This may be naive. However, it is more naive to think that £25,000 a year is a lot to ask for. To expand our service, we would still have to go and look for a similar amount of money each year. But, we would have gained a position of financial security to work from and the recognition that we were moving in the right direction would be priceless.

The role of teacher-in-charge, project manager and general dogs-body is extremely demanding and tiring. I am fortunate to have a loving family to support me, and a strong team at work who stand by me through the good and bad times. It is hard to continually have to explain the little bit you think you know about autism to other people who may want to listen, but have stresses and strains within their own situation. Knocking on fifty doors searching for the one that will open can be demoralising. The pride of finding yourself in a position where the service you lead is held up by some people to be a good one is equal in proportion to the stress one can feel because 'answers' are thin on the ground. It takes a perverse sense of discipline to complete the next charitable bid form for £1,000 when all you crave is to be mindless in front of *Coronation Street*. Nobody asked staff in The Resource to take on these additional roles and responsibilities. But, what are you supposed to do? Parents of children with ASDs have to take on many extra roles and responsibilities over and above those of families with non-autistic children. I may leave school and go home to work in the middle of the afternoon, but I only have the regular 'dark years' of two teenage daughters to contend with.

Parents of children in The Resource know they can phone school at any time. Most of them have my home phone number or that of my colleague. My phone can ring at 8 o'clock in the morning and 11 o'clock at night. Why does this happen? Because there may be no one else for people to turn to at these times. I am constantly amazed at the strength of some relationships I see when there is a youngster with an

ASD in the family. The strain on Mum and Dad is something I can only begin to imagine. However, there is a cost to providing this kind of service on my relationship with my wife and two daughters. There is no reason why they should be tolerant and understanding all of the time.

Nobody is irreplaceable. There are times when I have considered leaving this job and getting out of education altogether. The idea of a less stressful job that does not dominate a large chunk of life is sometimes very appealing. I still smile when some people talk with envy about the short working hours and long holidays that teachers get, but I am not sure how much longer that same smile can be worn. The next time a subject curriculum or exam criteria changes, I would like to sit with the people who make those decisions and explain a little bit about life on the front line. Initiative overload is what this phenomenon is called, but you can experience it at first hand by working within education. Recently, I saw a job advertised for an SEN (Special Educational Needs) Advisor in Sheffield. The salary started at £45,000 per annum, which is considerably more than I get paid and a total insult to support workers within specialist education. I am not saying that this post would be stress free, but it might be more possible to leave it behind at 5 p.m. It must be more difficult to become an 'advisory anorak'. It might be worth £45,000 a year to find out though.

I am sure that every worker in front line services of whatever kind, goes through regular periods of pessimism and yet, I cannot moan and groan for long. We all know that provisions, understanding and support for people with ASDs needs to improve. Tomorrow is another day and all that, and who knows, I might be lucky enough to meet someone like Hannah. People like Hannah inspire me to fill in the next bid form instead of watching my favourite soap opera.

Hannah came to King Ecgbert Resource from the same small special school as Shaun and Andrew. She was only the second girl we had ever taken. Her primary special school said that Hannah was very quiet; almost a self-elective mute if that is possible. Hannah's mum said that the only place she felt really comfortable enough to talk was at home, and there it was difficult to stop her speaking. Hannah was into all the same stuff as many other girls, fashion, magazines and music. She became a 'natural ally' of the female staff who attempted to make friends with Hannah. As a man, I was usually the butt of their jokes and jibes.

Hannah was meticulous in her academic work, but found most subjects that relied on literacy, interpretation and understanding of concepts, quite a challenge. She gave everything her best efforts and her smile lit up The Resource for five years. Hannah knew little about her autism at first and it was decided that any kind of formal counselling might place her under too much pressure. She watched other pupils in The Resource and I am certain we underestimated how much she was taking in. Over the years, Hannah began to ask questions about herself and other pupils in The Resource. These 'quiet chats' were not planned or recorded, and yet staff and Mum knew that Hannah was trying to piece together her own unique personality.

In her third year (when she was aged 13 to 14) Hannah wanted to have a weekly work placement at a hair and beauty shop. She was expressing a desire to follow this interest as a career. A colleague approached a hair salon, which was only about ten minutes' walk away from school. The manager was very enthusiastic. Hannah went for one morning a week for the following three years and also did her two-week block of work experience at the salon. Initially, support was given to Hannah and her employer. She quickly became a favourite with customers and other employees alike (all of whom were young girls just a little older than Hannah). Sometimes she would return to school at lunchtime and her hair was in braids. I took a couple of visitors to see Hannah at work and she was always busy, cleaning, making tea, or washing someone's hair. She also spent time helping on the desk. Her reference from this salon was the best I have ever read. It finished with the manager writing that Hannah could be successful in anything, but that she must choose hairdressing. Hannah gained some paid work at the salon over the summer holidays.

During her two GCSE years, Hannah studied hard. On entry to the school, her test scores amounted to a low 73 (with 100 being the national average). The school then predicted that Hannah would gain a G grade at GCSE English but fail in all other subjects. By this stage, staff were not paying too much attention to these predications anymore. Hannah's creative flair was utilised in GCSE Textiles. She had full support along with another pupil who had also opted for this technology subject. Part of the coursework was to design and make a fashionable bag. In total, this coursework counted for 60 per cent of the GCSE grade. Debra (our resident textiles expert at the time) acted as a superb guide and organiser for Hannah through the two years of the course. I know little about textiles and even less about women's bags, but what Hannah produced could have been sold in a trendy women's bag shop. It was all purple with beads, sequins and tassels. It gained a C grade. The simple task then was to prepare Hannah for the Textiles GCSE exam. Debra and the Textiles teacher taught Hannah well and by this time she wanted to keep this high grade.

Hannah came to school on results day. She nervously opened her envelope to discover that her efforts had been rewarded with a C grade in Textiles. Hannah also gained a D grade in English Language and French. She got two E grades in Science and a similar grade in English Literature. In Maths she managed a pass with an F grade. Not a person who welcomed hugs from over-exuberant male teachers, I had to jump up and down to contain my sheer pleasure for this 16-year-old. Hannah smiled serenely and said goodbye to me. I have not seen her since then.

Hannah gained a place on a hair and beauty course at Sheffield College and we alerted the autism team. We felt that she would need some support, but that they should take their lead from her. while still at school, Hannah applied for a Saturday job at a women's clothes store in Meadowhall. Hannah did not want anyone to know about her autism and asked for only minimal support from Glynis (someone she knew well from The Resource). Her mum caught the bus with Hannah for quite a while and Glynis met them so they could walk through Meadowhall together. This issue of a person not wanting other people to know about their ASD is a complex one. We have to be quite clear in our approach. Glynis explained to Hannah that she had to write about her autism on the application form (under the section about disability). It was explained that if Hannah was asked to do a job, but did not understand because of her autism, her employer might think it was because she could not, or would not do the task. However, if her employer were aware, they would understand that all

Hannah might need is a little support when learning a new task. A factor in our favour with this particular job was that the deputy manager of the store has a young son with an ASD. However, we did not know about that until later. Hannah got the job and has now been there for over a year. After a few months in the job, Glynis carried out some training on the use of public transport with Hannah. She has used public transport to and from work since then.

Hannah's tutor phoned me from college at the end of her first year. She had successfully completed a Level 1 GNVQ in Hair and Beauty and had been invited back to try for a Level 2. I have no doubts about her passing this with flying colours. Hannah had also been voted student of the year at her college site by the tutors and lecturers. I can almost picture the smile.

When Hannah left The Resource a year ago, she wrote a thank-you card to staff. Selfishly, I have kept it. I sometimes read it when things are tough. It reads:

To all the staff in The Resource.

I want to say a big thank you for all your support during the last five years. I will never forget the great times we've had and never forget you. I think you are all great support workers. I have learnt a lot while I've been in the resource. I've learnt how to communicate, to be more independent and how to be more confident. I have also learnt why I am in the Resource. I could not have done all this without all your help.

My Mum is grateful for all the support and help given throughout the years.

I will miss U all and come and visit in the future.

Lots of love,

HANNAH.

If I want to see Hannah again, my best bet is to drag some poor unsuspecting female into the clothes shop where she works at Meadowhall (I suppose I could take my wife, which might prevent me from being locked up). Becoming a special needs advisor (even at £45,000 a year), or getting out of education altogether suddenly appears less attractive. And, it is all Hannah's fault.

CHAPTER 8

Autism and Society

I am a teacher, not a commentator on the current state of society. One of the hardest things for me to do since co-writing our first book is to speak in public about what we do (and control my bowel movements at the same time). However, what we see in our school society for me is just a reflection of what is happening in a wider sense. This wider picture has to be taken into account in the work we do. Unless we attempt to develop some understanding of what is happening beyond the school gates, trying to get the best out of people with ASDs whom we work alongside is almost impossible. How many times do you hear adults say something like: 'I wouldn't want to be a teenager today'? In the next breath they might also point to increased leisure activities, greater wealth and a wider range of choices that teenagers have today. Yet, there seems to be some acknowledgment that they are in some way under more pressure than were previous generations of young people.

Added to this pressure, there seems to be a greater emphasis on children becoming young adults at a much earlier age. It is not difficult to see where this shortening of childhood comes from. Teenagers today have more disposable income than previous generations of young people. The 'markets' have realised this and are more than happy to cater for it. Take a look in any teenage girl magazine (if you are a father, it is probably a good idea to sit down first), and look at how many companies target our young teenage children. There is make-up, trainers, music CDs, jewellery and mobile phones to buy. The 'role models' that are offered to our young teenagers seem to come from one tall, thin and stick-like mould. I do not recognise the beautiful teenagers on TV programmes that are aimed at our young people and I certainly do not remember looking like that.

Put over 1,000 young people into a secondary school and it is not difficult to see that these institutions have become places where a large percentage of children just survive. Many do not 'fit' the human model that is touted by the magazines and on TV. Our school is successful in getting about 55 per cent of children through at least five GCSEs with C grades or above. This figure has not altered a great deal from the school being full of predominantly white, middle-class children, to a school that takes a much wider range of academic ability and over 20 per cent of pupils who come from cultural backgrounds that are not white, English. That is good for any school and the teachers deserve great credit. Our Sixth Form now has a much wider range of courses, other than just the pure A Levels.

For a small number of pupils who just cannot cope in a mainstream secondary school, there are options for them to do something more vocational. However, for the 40 per cent of pupils who may find academic work a challenge, I would still have to question what is on offer from the education process. We still try to squeeze nine or ten GCSEs out of them, and wonder why some start to behave in more challenging ways, or simply do not attend school as often. If a teenager shows signs of becoming disaffected in any way, schools do not seem well equipped or flexible enough to meet his or her needs. It does not appear to matter how much emphasis a school places on other areas in which children can succeed, such as sport, music and dance, the pressure always returns to academic success. The publication of league tables does not help this clamber for academic success and I can easily imagine the pressure that head teachers (and heads of departments) must be under on results day for GCSE and A Levels. The amount of testing and examinations that our children have to go through is high and, for some, so is the cost to their formative years.

In the media, our teenagers are seeing graphic examples of intolerance, hatred and violence on a daily basis. People are prepared to harm others in the name of religion and ideological differences. Sadly, this is nothing new. However, we are increasingly bombarded with these images in our daily lives through the expansion and intrusion of the mass media. Our teenagers witness different races of people struggling to live side by side. They see the most powerful nation in the world using force to invade other countries. Negotiation, understanding and compromise appear to have been replaced with firepower, innocent civilian deaths and suicide bombers. People are murdered because of minor disagreements. In sport, people on the terraces barrack black football players with monkey noises and throw banana skins. The authorities appear to do little about it. The pursuit of revenue for TV companies is more influential than the voices of reason.

In our schools, Head Teachers have gained new powers to search pupils who may be carrying offensive weapons such as knives. There appears to be a growing culture of fear, hostility and violence, which is fed and stirred by the gutter press. It should be of little surprise when this culture is reflected in our schools. It would be easy to let this sense of pessimism affect our work as we wonder what effect our small efforts could possibly have on society. It would be easy to start quoting older and more extreme philosophical ideas about the state of man and democracy, such as Thomas Hobbes whose famous quote about life being 'solitary, poor, nasty, brutish and short' (*Leviathan* 1651) will probably re-appear in some of the less savoury newspapers in the coming months.

At the same time, the gap between the richest and poorest sections of our community has continued to grow in the last ten years. A report in August 2004 by the Institute for Public Policy Research stated that Britain is far from being a progressive or just society. Levels of child poverty continue to surpass those of many of our more successful European partners, and inequalities in income, wealth and well-being remain stubbornly high (IPPR 2004). The report points out that the gap between white and ethnic minority employment rates has widened. However, between 1990 and 2000, the proportion of wealth owned by the richest 10 per cent of the population increased from 47 per cent to 54 per cent. Life is certainly not 'short and brutish' for this highly privileged 10 per cent of the population.

It is from this increasingly harsh background beyond the school gates, that staff in The Resource are trying to get the message across to mainstream teenagers that it is 'good to be different'. Being different is cool and should be the source of celebration, not finger point-ing. Given the turbulent times in which we are living, it is perhaps not surprising that it is proving to be an increasingly difficult message to get heard. Being different is certainly not cool at the moment and this extends way beyond autism. Ask any overweight teenager about their experiences at school. The overwhelming majority of our teenagers are railroaded though an inflexible education system where differ-ences are not easily accommodated, therefore the message seems to be that it is easier to 'fit in' and conform, rather than stand out against the crowd. The majority of pupils in The Resource do stand out as being different, and so staff see these potential conflicts on a daily basis. Some pupils in The Resource will rightly make no apology for their differences. However, these differences can have negative con-sequences for some pupils with an ASD who might have to work extra hard in lessons to 'cover' their autism (at a potentially high per-sonal cost) or just wish that this 'thing' could be surgically removed.

One of our Y11 pupils (aged 16) who has just finished school spent the first four years in The Resource hating his autism. He threw himself into school drama productions and even tried playing cricket after school. He was desperate to fit in and be accepted. Every time something went wrong or he made a mistake, or he failed to get a leading role in drama, he blamed his autism. His lack of girlfriends was easily explained, by his autism. He tried to be funny to make friends and he tried being quiet and blending into the background. The more he tried to be the same as everyone else, the more he made himself stand out as being different. He largely gave up on the aca-demic side of school. He could not wait to leave school because he felt that he could make a fresh start and no one would know about his autism. He had counselling and anger management lessons, and a spell of work experience at Tescos for one year. Nothing appeared to be working. In his final year, he began to experience some success in two subject areas (English and Resistant Materials). He began to believe that academic success was one way to gain acceptance. He saw exams as a 'level playing field' where his hard work and effort could gain him some acknowledgement. He worked harder than any-one I have ever seen in a final year at school. His confidence began to grow. He began to dream (along with staff) of two or three C grades at GCSE in his favourite subject areas. He worked hard at the others. He got his results: three C grades and a couple of Ds. These grades represent minor miracles, as he was predicted E grades across all subjects when he began his secondary education. More importantly, he is looking forward to getting away from school and into college where he has decided to be open and clear about his disability. His attitude is that he will support people at college to understand more about autism, and will work with people who accept him for who he is, and stuff the rest (in the nicest possible way, of course). It is a good start to the rest of his journey through life and there were many times when I felt he would not take this first step.

In addition to all these external pressures on teenagers and schools, our social commentators cannot decide whether inclusion and access for pupils with additional needs is a good idea or not. Baroness Mary Warnock, whose work and reports on education over twenty years ago engineered the move towards statementing and access and inclusion for disabled children within mainstream schools, has now apparently changed her mind. Access and inclusion is only one area of life where she appears to have carried out a full u-turn. The language she uses has to be excused because of changing times with which she has clearly not kept up. She describes the movement of children out of special schools into mainstream as a 'disastrous legacy', causing 'confusion of which children are the casualties' (Warnock 2005). She points to the increase in Statements as being wasteful and bureaucratic. It is true that there has been an increase in the number of pupils gaining Statements over the past ten years, from about 2 per cent of children to 3 per cent. This should not surprise us given the small drift of pupils from special schools into mainstream education. It is the only protection in law that these children have to gain access to the support they need. People have given blood, sweat and tears to win these rights for some of society's most vulnerable children. Warnock's attempts to discredit gains made in access and inclusion in education over the past twenty years would go largely unnoticed except for the fact that they will always be used by commentators with other agendas. Her comments were followed by articles in the press denouncing the closure of special schools and the damage done to mainstream pupils by the inclusion of disabled pupils in 'regular' schools. Some people in power began to shout for the halt to the closure of special schools and as usual, they missed the most important points.

The fact that special schools have not been closed in their thousands should come as no surprise. Warnock was suggesting greater inclusion and access at a time when some commentators looked down on special schools as simply places of care. Nothing could be further from the truth today. The problem is that employers and society in general still consider pupils from special schools to be, in some way, second best. A small percentage of special schools have closed over the past ten years. The move towards further closures must be resisted at the moment because mainstream schools are not given the necessary funding to be able to meet the many and varied support needs of more vulnerable pupils. Mainstream secondary schools have to adapt and become more flexible in their approaches to pupils with additional needs before such children will be well catered for. The move towards greater inclusion and access in mainstream education is the equivalent to the move towards 'care in the community' in the field of mental health. These ideas will work for some people and not for others. It should never be seen as a way of saving money. Care in the community needed greater investment and cohesive thinking, the same as access and inclusion for pupils with additional needs does. Investment in people is never wasted.

What worries me just as much as a lack of investment in people, are groups who advocate total access and inclusion within a single educational system. It is not that I can disagree with the sentiment of a single education system in which all children play, learn and live together. These groups make it almost impossible for anyone but the most extreme bigot to disagree with them. However, even from a white, liberal middle-class background, I find the principles involved in total inclusive education to be shortsighted, idealistic and out of touch with reality. The simple truth is that some children need and will benefit from inclusion into a mainstream setting, and others will thrive and develop more successfully within a segregated provision. This is true for autism as it is for other disabilities. Once this simple truth is accepted (and we stop wasting so much time debating the issues involved) we can get on with the far more important job of ensuring that the quality of education delivered in both settings is of the highest possible standard. The vast majority of special schools in Sheffield are excellent, just the same as the vast majority of mainstream schools in the area. With a range of needs within ASDs comes the need for a wide range of provisions within education. It is time to move on from this dead-end of a debate about mainstream versus special.

The factor that has in some way 'muddied the waters' of access and inclusion is the greater push for pupils with challenging behaviour to be within mainstream schools. This includes pupils whom Head Teachers are 'encouraged' to take, knowing that they may have been excluded from other schools because of a failure to cope. while the education system does its best to alienate a large proportion of pupils, the fact that there are more children in mainstream who exhibit challenging behaviour has undoubtedly caused problems, which have not yet been solved (or sometimes, even addressed.) In 2004, an OFSTED report pointed out that admission of pupils with social and behavioural problems into mainstream schools is proving to be the hardest test of the inclusion framework. In the report, David Bell (Chief Inspector) highlighted this issue as the one where conflicts between meeting individual needs, and the efficient education of other children, are the most difficult to reconcile (OFSTED 2004). The teaching unions are right to point to a lack of resources in this area.

A lot of these pupils need much more intensive social and life skills teaching than can be offered in a mainstream setting. They need an adapted curriculum to suit their needs. We get to know some mainstream pupils who might be considered to have challenging behaviour because they happily use our resource base at lunchtime. It is rare for them to cause staff any difficulties. However, I am not convinced that I would like to try to 'reach' some of these pupils within the confines of a History or French lesson. There is also a lack of combined efforts between the special and mainstream sector. Some pupils with challenging behaviour need a mixed curriculum that can only be offered by spending some time in both sectors. The vocational training in both sectors needs a radical overhaul. It seems to be a modern concept that the numbers of students at universities are increasing to satisfy the financial greed of such institutions, while at the same time, it is difficult to get the services of a good plumber or carpenter. At the expense of sounding old and decrepit, I am not sure how many more young people actually need degrees in Media Studies.

Teachers at King Ecgbert School can generally manage the difficult behaviour that might be displayed sometimes by a few pupils in The Resource. They are experienced and trained within the field of autism, and most importantly, they have a team of staff to turn to for advice, support and comfort. Teachers know they are never far away from someone who will try to understand, and has more than likely been through similar difficulties in other lessons. Teachers also know that there is somewhere to send a pupil from The Resource if it looks like there could be potential difficulties in a lesson. They also know that other pupils can work in The Resource alongside pupils with ASDs if this is appropriate for a particular lesson. They have options and choices within their own classroom and subject area. Within this positive and empowering atmosphere where individual need and flexibility are key principles, teachers are far more likely to 'push back the boundaries' themselves and experience success which can then be further built on. This transfer of knowledge and expertise between 'mainstream' and 'special' is the bedrock of success for pupils with ASDs at King Ecgbert School. Once a school is working well in terms of being 'autism friendly', staff have to increasingly move beyond the school gates to look for the next battlegrounds. They are many and never far away.

One way for educational success to be achieved is for provisions like The Resource to go 'over numbers'. This is not as disastrous as it sounds because of the funding formula that Sheffield LEA employs for such provisions within mainstream schools. It is a fixed amount of money per pupil, per year. This means that the increased income to the school can be used for additional staff within The Resource. Assuming we can be relatively successful with a proportion of these twenty-eight pupils, other children who require higher levels of support can be catered for. We can also offer some degree of service to mainstream pupils who are on the spectrum thus cementing our partnership with the school even more. It also enables staff to tackle the much more difficult job of attempting to encourage society and key people (such as employers) to become more autism friendly within the confines of the period of history in which we find ourselves.

It is relatively easy in a blinkered way for anoraks to agree on what needs to be achieved over the next ten years. It could be demonstrated in a naive and straightforward way as a triad of improvements as opposed to a triad of impairments:

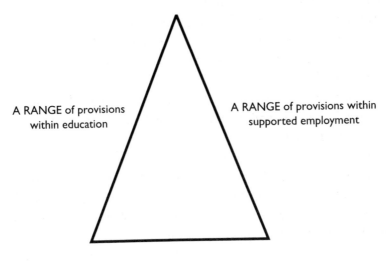

Figure 8.1 A triad of improvements

This range of options would ensure that society began to see the strengths of people with ASDs on a much more regular basis. It is still not rocket science and there are two major tasks for professionals to achieve in order to make progress towards reaching these goals. There is no need any more for autism to be the hidden disability.

First, and perhaps unfairly, our main priority has got to be to pre-pare the young people with whom we work to take their place in society to whatever degree they can achieve. The adaptability and understanding of self and others we all strive for in someone on the spectrum has to be pursued above everything else. All the GCSEs in the world will not be enough unless there is a growing self-awareness and understanding of others, however basic that might be. Every young person we work alongside has got to be considered as an advocate for the next generation. We have to use every possible way forward to demonstrate on a daily basis that (with a little support) someone with an ASD can make sense of the neurotypical world, and that it is worth getting to know better. Not an easy task given what is happening beyond the school gates. Given the conflicts and growing violence in the UK and around the world, some pupils in The Resource have periods of feeling angry, confused, but above all, frightened. In this respect and many others, they are no different to their mainstream peers. Issues in the news that cause high anxiety levels have to be discussed within The Resource. It is vital to talk about the wider issues in society and the concerns and fears that our teenagers have. Safe places and times have to be found for this, otherwise we run the risk of increasing stress levels and a loss of focus. This places a huge responsibility (and burden) on young people with ASDs to take the lead in the second and much more difficult area of work.

Society to me appears less tolerant and understanding of 'differences' than it was twenty or thirty years ago. We are supporting young people with ASDs to be ready for a society that is changing at a faster pace than ever before. Hopefully, larger numbers of people with ASDs are going to be taking their place in society and shoulder the responsibilities in teaching others about their strengths, and which areas they might find more of a challenge. This, and subsequent generations of young adults have got to be prepared to cope with people who will potentially misinterpret and misunderstand them. They have to be ready to work alongside people who may have less time and are under more pressure. In this respect, going through five years of mainstream secondary education could be considered quite an appropriate learning experience. The difference will hopefully be that increasing numbers of these young people with ASDs will emerge from secondary and college education with their self-esteem very much intact. Mistakes will continue to be inevitable as they are for neurotypical people. The young people will be moving towards less travelled paths, and so we have to be there in some form, to continue guiding, explaining, re-asserting and re-assuring. We can then continue to learn about what needs to be tackled next so that improvements in services are really ongoing. It has to be a partnership that naturally influences and convinces increasing numbers of people to see that there are gains to be made for all involved. At a time when a lot of what appears to be happening is based on conflict, misunderstanding and confrontation, this is not going to be easy to achieve. That means we have to celebrate each success, however small they might appear to others. Workers on the front line have to jump for joy when they see a light at the end of the tunnel (and hope it is not a train coming the other way).

I smile inside when people mention Andrew and his success at Sainsbury's, or Shaun working as an administrative officer. In our staff bulletin at school I sometimes write about their endeavours along with all of the ex-pupils from The Resource at King Ecgbert School. People are rightly proud of our ex-pupils like Shaun and Andrew, not so much because they are doing a good job even though they are autistic. They are proud of them simply because they are doing a good job. The investment is paying dividends. Within Sainsbury's, Andrew is just Andrew. He has broken new ground within this supermarket and with the other employees with whom he has come into contact. When the human resources manager who was instrumental in getting Andrew the job moved from that store to work in a nearby Sainsbury's, she wrote and told me. She also pointed out in her letter that the new store she was going to would welcome people with ASDs on work placements and in paid employment positions. I can live with that. When the audience sees Matthew or other pupils from The Resource in the school drama production, they are just being good actors, along with the rest of the cast. In key areas, and to a large extent, their autism is now secondary to who they are.

Each member of staff in The Resource, at college and at Meadowhall, celebrates this discovery of self and self-confidence. When our pupils want to succeed at school or at college, and when our young adults in work or on placements want to do a first rate job, then staff know that as long as some level of support continues, the potential for these individuals is unlimited. All they need is the opportunity to contribute to society. Letting them in cannot possibly do any harm.

And our lottery bid? Three months after it was re-submitted, we are still waiting to hear whether it has been successful or not. A second bid to another charitable foundation has been rewarded with £20,000. However, this would only be given to us if the lottery bid fails. If the decisions by these faceless people are delayed for many more months, our small charity will fold. Glynis will be unable to carry on at Meadowhall, and we would not be able to expand our supported employment into Sheffield city centre. Sometimes I get through a day at work and realise that I have not even thought about this, or the ludicrous position in which it leaves us. We have to think about 'fallback' positions in case the bid fails. Our website now has something called a shopping link. Items that are purchased though this shopping link on the website gain our charity a small percentage of the price. Perhaps this kind of nonsense (apart from smelling of desperation) moves us nearer to the day when The Resource could gain sponsorship from a large fast food chain. Who knows where it could end?

Eddie recently asked me what would happen to The Resource if I got run over by a bus ('no offence', he quickly added). I told him there would be people to take over from me and that the work and the support would carry on. He wanted to know who he would phone when he felt alone. That is where Mr R. McDonald could not possibly help. With adequate levels of the right quality support, Eddie and his peers should not have to worry about individual professionals and what would happen if they were not there anymore. They should be too busy pushing back the boundaries and supporting other people to understand more about ASDs and individual human beings. I am certain that this will happen more often because of the tireless work of parents and professionals on the front line. This leaves little time to persuade the people who make decisions about investment in people to look at what Eddie and his peers are achieving. But, time has to be found. If not, all we are left with is a vague hope that things will get better. And that is not enough.

References

Barnard, J., Harvey, V., Prior, A. and Potter, D. (2001) *Ignored or Ineligible*. London: National Autistic Society.

Broach, S., Camgoz, S., Heather, C., Owen, G., Potter, D. and Prior, A. (2003) *Autism: Rights in Reality*. London: National Autistic Society.

Frith, U. (1991) *Autism and Asperger Syndrome*. Cambridge: Cambridge University Press.

Grandin, T. (1999) 'Choosing the right job for people with Autism or Asperger Syndrome'. www.autism.org/temple/jobs.html, accessed August 2005.

Haddon, M. (2004) *The Curious Incident of the Dog in the Night-time*. London: Vintage.

Harker, M. and King, N. (2004) *Tomorrow's Big Problem: Housing Options For people With Autism*. London. National Autistic Society.

Hesmondhalgh, M. and Breakey, C. (2001) *Access and Inclusion for Children with Autistic Spectrum Disorders: 'Let Me In'*. London: Jessica Kingsley Publishers.

Howlin, P. (1997) *Autism: Preparing for Adulthood*. London: Routledge.

Institute for Public Policy Research (IPPR) (2004) 'A decade of tackling poverty, but Britain's far from a fair society.' www.ippr.org.uk/pressreleases/?id=810, accessed August 2005.

Jackson, L. (2002) *Freaks, Geeks and Asperger Syndrome: A User Guide To Adolescence*. London: Jessica Kingsley Publishers.

Knapp, M. and Jarbrink, K. (2001) 'The economic impact of Autism in Britain'. *Autism 5*, 1, 7–22.

Neill, A.S. (1968) *Summerhill*. London: Pelican.

OFSTED (2004) http://news.bbc.co.uk/1/hi/education/3734370.stm, accessed August 2005.

Peeters, T. and Gillberg, C. (1999) *Autism: Medical and Educational Aspects*. London: Whurr Publishers.

Rogers, C. (1983) *Freedom To Learn*. Ohio: Charles E. Merrill Publishing Co.

Sainsbury, C. (2000) *Martian In The Playground: Understanding the Schoolchild with Asperger's Syndrome*. London: Lucky Duck Publishing Ltd.

Warnock, M. (2005) http://news.bbc.co.uk/1/hi/education/4071122.stm, accessed August 2005.